A Gentle Touch

A Gentle Touch

Christians and Mental Illness

John Ting

A GENTLE TOUCH
Copyright © 2014 John Ting

Published by Graceworks Private Limited
22 Sin Ming Lane
#04-76 Midview City
Singapore 573969
E-mail: enquiries@graceworks.com.sg
Website: www.graceworks.com.sg

Ng Bee Ying's testimony on pages 43 to 47 was previously published in
the August–September 2003 issue of Impact Magazine and is reprinted with
kind permission from Impact Christian Communications Ltd, Singapore.

A CIP record for this book is available from the National Library Board, Singapore

ISBN: 978-981-07-7729-6

3 4 5 6 7 8 9 10 · 23 22 21 20 19

Contents

Foreword

Those who suffer from mental illness and distress often suffer alone and struggle to understand what they are going through. Personal anguish is further exacerbated by the social stigma commonly attached to mental illness — as if mental illness is a sign of weakness of character or religious faith. There are still many myths floating around regarding mental illness that prevent sufferers from gaining understanding and those around them from offering empathy and help.

This book offers an honest and poignant look at common forms of mental illness and provides information, insight, comfort and hope. Written by Reverend John Ting who has had personal experience of depression and who has, from that experience, gained much understanding and insight from reading and training, this book describes in a realistic way how people suffer from conditions such as depression, anxiety disorders, panic attacks and addictive behaviour, and how they can find help and encouragement.

Particularly helpful in this book are the personal stories told by Reverend Ting and others he has helped (as a pastor and counsellor) and the biblical reflections shared by the author. The stories are measured in months and years, suggesting that often there is no magical cure; however there is help available for recovery as patients work through their struggles and illness. Dealing with mental illness is a very human thing, and suffering and recovering from mental illness brings out what it means to be human. It helps us to understand that we are embodied beings. Our life is embedded in our biological makeup and functioning; we are deeply influenced by significant experiences and relationships, particularly in childhood; we struggle with the increasing stresses and strains of modern life and we learn good and bad habits of coping; we operate according to good and bad scripts we have learned; we are affected by spiritual realities, and our faith plays a central role in how we live in this personal, biological, social and spiritual milieu.

Belief and relief are connected, as shown by the sermons and biblical reflections found in this book. What we know about God and how we relate with Him have significant effects on how we live. Our faith has redemptive and therapeutic effects. This reminds us of how the apostle Paul frankly shared: "we were harassed at every turn – conflicts on the outside, fears within. But God, who comforts the downcast, comforted us..." (2 Corinthians 7.5–6).

A Gentle Touch brings a holistic perspective, taking into consideration the different dimensions of being human and how these are all rooted in the reality of God. It is written with deep pastoral empathy and a living and profound faith. Both sufferers and those who help them will find in this book comforting insights and hopeful pointers. I hope that this book will be widely read as it helps dispel many myths about mental illness, raises awareness and offers a realistic and most helpful perspective.

Bishop Emeritus Dr Robert Solomon
The Methodist Church in Singapore

Preface

Originally I was asked to adapt the Mental Health First Aid (Singapore) training programme for use with churches. The adaptation took the form of a supplementary 'companion' to the MHFA (S) manual. The companion assumed, as given, the material in the manual and followed its chapter headings. Subsequently, it was decided not to restrict its distribution to only participants in the MHFA (S) training programme but to make it available to the wider Christian community as a standalone book.

I have written this book from a pastor's perspective rather than the perspective of a mental health professional. I address various questions Christians may have about mental illness. For example, how can we distinguish between demonism and schizophrenia? Does trusting God for healing mean the non-use of medication? Can a committed Christian who sincerely seeks to trust God experience clinical depression? Commit suicide? Suffer from anxiety disorders?

I want Christian laypeople to have a better understanding of mental illnesses. Thus I have added 'flesh' to names and terms by incorporating anecdotes and testimonies, including my own. As a sufferer of mental illness in the form of depression, I have been able to empathise with fellow sufferers, especially those with mood disorders. This has led me to read more about mental illnesses. In my pastoral ministry, I have also come into contact with people with mental illness, especially depression. All this has helped fill gaps in my knowledge of mental illness and its treatment, and facilitated reflection from a biblical perspective.

My prayer is that this book will help Christians when they face the issue of mental illness and come into contact with the mentally ill. Sadly, many Christians have myths and misconceptions about mental illness. Hopefully, this book will help dispel these myths and misconceptions as well as positively inform and educate.

John Ting

Acknowledgements

Special thanks to Angelina Chan (Senior Consultant Psychiatrist, Trauma Recovery and Corporate Solutions [TRaCS], Changi General Hospital) and Jeannie Koh (former manager and senior counsellor, NUS Counselling Services). They 'arrowed' and encouraged me to write this book and responded to my requests for feedback and information with patience and professional expertise despite their busy schedules.

I am grateful to Melody, 'Michael' and Jeffrey for contributing their testimonies and Bee Ying and Harris for permission to include their previously published testimonies.

I want to express my thanks to Bishop Robert Solomon for his very kind, thoughtful and encouraging Foreword.

I also want to thank my editor and publisher Bernice Lee of Graceworks who saw the value of this book and readily undertook the task of making it available to the Christian public.

Finally, my thanks to the Lord for His enabling grace and for the deep privilege of writing this book.

Introduction

A Holistic View of Mental Health

Men and women are physical, emotional, mental, psychological, social and spiritual beings. Each dimension may influence and be influenced by other dimensions. A holistic approach to healing needs to be aware of these different dimensions, including the spiritual dimension or realm, as objective realities. In some periods of a person's mental illness, the spiritual dimension may not be the most significant. Let me draw an analogy. While we will want to pray for someone experiencing an asthmatic attack, we will also understand the priority need for the sufferer to use his Ventolin inhaler or nebuliser. Similarly with mental illness. A person experiencing an acute bipolar episode, for example, may need a mood stabiliser, anti-psychotic medication and possibly an antidepressant even as we pray for the sufferer. When the sufferer has become more stabilised through psychiatric treatment, spiritual resources will then be appropriate and helpful.

Furthermore, a holistic view of mental health means the process of healing will rarely be the sole domain of any one discipline, whether psychiatry, psychotherapy, pastoral care or the loving support of family and friends. In certain phases of a person's mental illness the focus may narrow. For example, when a person is severely delusional, the focus will need to be on psychiatric treatment. When the sufferer has stabilised, psychotherapy, pastoral care and the loving support of family and friends may then contribute to the ongoing healing process. The different testimonies in this book all bear witness to the holistic nature of the healing process or 'synergy' as one testimony termed it.

Counselling and Therapy in a Church Context

Preaching and teaching should counsel as well as open up the way for people to seek counsel

People ought to find themselves being 'counselled' as they listen and respond to faithful expository preaching which expounds the Word and applies it aptly and relevantly to people's lives. Dr Martyn Lloyd-Jones in his book *Preaching and Preachers*,[1] makes this point very strongly: "The preaching of the Gospel from the pulpit, applied by the Holy Spirit to the individuals who are listening, has been the means of dealing with personal problems of which I as the preacher knew nothing until people came to me at the end of the service saying, 'I want to thank you for that sermon because if you had known I was there and the exact nature of my problem, you could not have answered my various questions more perfectly.'"[2]

Three tiers of counselling in churches

Arising from a model of counselling for churches suggested by Larry Crabb[3] I believe we can speak of three tiers of counselling that can be present in churches.

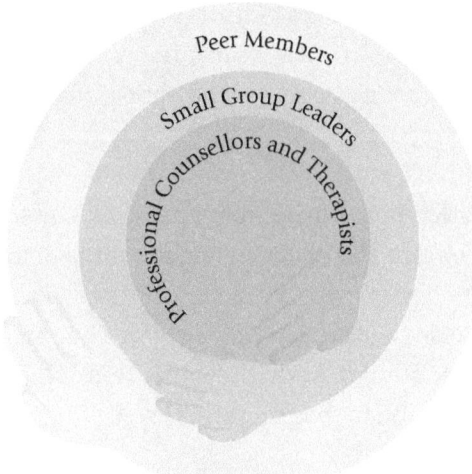

a.   There ought to be mutual care and encouragement for every member. In my book, *Living Biblically in Marriage and at Home*,[4] I wrote the following with regard to issues faced by singles in churches:

> One of my favourite songs is 'Jesus take me as I am, I can come no other way.' I believe there are those in our churches who wish they could say to others, 'Brothers and sisters, take me as I am. Allow me to take off my mask. Please do not stereotype me. Do not project onto me struggles I do not have. Or, do not be too quick to judge and dismiss me because of the struggles I do have. Walk alongside me as my brother, my sister. Encourage me in my walk with the Lord as I want to encourage you in your walk. You with your joys and struggles and I with mine, some similar, some different.'[5]

I believe what I wrote in regard to singleness applies across the board. If this kind of attitude and milieu were to become an integral part of a church's culture, there would be fewer people with more serious mental health issues. The issues would be addressed at an early stage and, hopefully, prevented from growing.

b.   At the next tier there will be problems, issues and struggles where mutual peer care and encouragement will be inadequate. Here, small group leaders with more maturity and experience may be able to provide the needed level of counselling and help. Church leaders, especially pastors with further training and experience, can be called upon to counsel at this level.

c.   There will be situations where the seriousness of the problem requires referral to professional counsellors and therapists. Ideally, professional counsellors and therapists can exercise a team ministry with pastors in the care of church members. On occasion, I have asked to see a church member's psychiatrist (with the permission of the church member except for special cases). I ask the psychiatrist for advice on how I, as a pastor, can best help the member and also what advice I should give to the member's concerned family, friends and members of his or her small group.

Client-Centred Therapy? Yes and No!

Yes in that counselling and counsellor serve the client — not the other way round. No in that we are not to apply the standard secular counselling principle of counselling only within the framework of the client's worldview and value system. While we should not impose our biblical worldview and values on the client, our counselling should nevertheless presume them. The framework that shapes our counselling should be God's framework as revealed in Scripture, not the client's framework, if unbiblical. This is God's world and the Bible contains the 'Maker's instructions' telling us how we will best function according to God's intention and purpose for humankind.

> The framework that shapes our counselling should be God's framework as revealed in Scripture.

Believing Prayer for 'Miraculous' Healing vs Therapy and Medication

Miraculous healing?

People have been healed directly by God at healing services and, apart from healing services, in answer to believing prayer. In the early seventies a very senior Singaporean police officer took his teenage daughter who had leukaemia to the USA for Kathryn Kuhlman's healing service. He told me he personally witnessed miraculous healing such as legs extending. He also told me that his daughter was not healed of her illness and died later back in Singapore. Kathryn Kuhlman herself, I believe, died of an illness.

The late Professor Khoo Oon Teik, formerly Professor of Clinical Medicine at the University of Singapore, medically documented using 'before and after' X-rays people who were healed directly by God in answer to believing prayer. A member of my Sydney church, a medical doctor, recently testified to me that he and a few others, while on a mission trip, prayed for hearing to be restored to a group of twelve deaf men. Eleven of them were healed of their deafness. I believe there are many similar testimonies of 'miraculous' healing. There have also been many people prayed for who were not healed.

Healing in the atonement?

A number of today's charismatics (and perhaps non-charismatics) believe that if a person is not willfully committing or harbouring sin and has the requisite faith, he or she will be healed. Behind this belief is an understanding of 'healing in the atonement' based on Isaiah 53.5, "...and by his wounds we are healed..." The verse begins with "he was pierced for our transgressions, he was crushed for our iniquities...". Just as the atonement means we can expect forgiveness of sins the very moment we confess them (1 John 1.9) so, analogously, we can expect healing of illness the moment we exercise faith and claim healing on the basis of Jesus' wounds on the Cross. I do not believe in 'healing in the atonement' understood this way but I can understand why many people do. This understanding may sound very persuasive and even 'obvious'.

In fact, there are those who would go further and say it is either medicine or faith, thus putting the two in opposition to each other. In response, I refer to 1 Timothy 5.23, "Stop drinking only water, and use a little wine because of your stomach and your *frequent* illnesses" (emphasis mine). Wine has some medicinal value. On my doctor's advice, I sometimes drink wine for my triglycerides. Furthermore, wine being fermented and processed, would have had less harmful bacteria than the untreated water of Paul's day. I reason from this verse that if Paul believed in 'healing in the atonement' he might have advised Timothy differently and he would not have expected Timothy to have frequent illnesses. It is possible Paul's 'thorn in the flesh' (2 Corinthians 12.7–8) was an illness, though not necessarily so. God is the source of healing. Sometimes He chooses to heal directly in answer to believing prayer and other times He heals through the use of medicine. In Timothy's case it was wine. In my case it was prayer, bypass surgery and medicine for my heart; and prayer, surgery, hormone therapy and radiotherapy for my prostate cancer. Believing prayer and medical procedures are not mutually exclusive. It is not a case of either believing prayer or medical procedures but believing prayer and medical procedures! And, as I have implied above, sometimes God's way is believing prayer without medical procedures.

A Person with Chronic Schizophrenia Shares His Experience

Harris Ng suffered from chronic schizophrenia for many years. He recounts his experiences in his encouraging and inspiring book *Recovered Grace: Schizophrenia.* He tells us he had three relapses. This is Harris' own account of his second relapse.[6]

> Things went well for a year until a friend asked me whether I believed in miracle healing. It was in the good old year, 1978. "If you are healed, you need not be dependent on your medication anymore. You need not go back to Adam Road hospital for your medical appointments every four weeks. Don't you know you look well to all of us? You can also save a lot of money as the medication and consultation is not cheap!"
>
> On hearing what he had so helpfully suggested, I was ready to take the plunge. "There is no harm in trying..." Or so I thought. Unfortunately, this friend of mine seemed not to have understood the nature of my illness. He was all out trying to offer help to me. I could see he was sincere, but the result that followed was shocking.
>
> He took me to a huge gathering on an open field. Thousands of people were gathered there that night. A speaker was proclaiming the power of prayer in miracle healing. He spoke with a booming voice. The

speakers installed at every corner made it ever the more overwhelming. Drowned in the loud music, songs and noises, my mind whirled and spun. Trepidation filled my soul as I witnessed the long queue leading to the speaker. One by one he laid hands on them. A man stood up from a wheel chair and tried to walk. My friend urged me, "Join the queue." When my turn came, the speaker proclaimed, "Rebuke the devil! Rebuke the powers of darkness! Be healed and let God forgive you." Then followed a disturbing ring of unknown languages. For a newcomer, it was rather intimidating. There was extreme fear in me and a chill ran down my spine. I felt like I was about to faint. It was as if an electric current had gone through me. "Now you may go in peace. You are delivered and healed. Amen!"

I left the speaker with a blank in my mind, not knowing what to do and what had exactly happened. The crowd was so huge that there was no time to entertain everyone. I left the crowd, accompanied by my friend. On the way home, he said, "You are now completely healed. You need not be dependent on your medication anymore. God's mercy is upon you. The powers of Satan have been taken away and you are now free from your sickness." I stopped my medication without asking a question. I went around rather happily, believing in the words of my friend and the speaker for about a month. After that the thoughts came streaming into my mind again. Mine was a case of chronic schizophrenia. On hindsight, I understood that it was not a case of Satanic possession, though others may disagree with me on that point. The thoughts darted left and right, positive and negative. What was happening to me again? ...

It was my third breakdown and second relapse. The diagnosis cleared me of being under evil possession. It stated clearly that it was a case of mental illness (schizophrenia)…I do believe in miracles. Jesus had performed many of them as recorded in the Gospels…We need to understand that God can make use of the hands of a doctor to heal the sick, and so medical healing is not contrary to miracle healing or faith healing.

Further Reading

Gordon Fee, *The Disease of the Health and Wealth Gospels* (Vancouver, Canada: Regent College Publishing, 1985).

Harris Ng, *Recovered Grace: Schizophrenia* (Singapore: Harris Ng, 2005).

Patricia Yap, Daryl Chow, Sharon Lu, Brenda Lee (eds.), *Mind This Voice: The Write to Recovery* (Singapore: Institute of Mental Health, 2011).

Psychosis

Demonism vs Psychosis? Therapy vs Deliverance?[7]

Obsessed with demons?

There are Christians who seem obsessed with demons in that they 'see' demons everywhere. There seems to be no room for 'natural' explanations of events and happenings which appear to be out of character or out of the ordinary. These are quickly attributed to the demonic. An 'out-of-character' outburst of temper may be attributed to a 'spirit of anger' which needs to be cast out rather than attributed, for example, to stress and tension. It is true that out-of-character thinking and behaviour may be demonic in origin, but not necessarily so.

In June 1986, I was a supervisor at the Family Help Centre, an adjunct ministry of the Luis Palau Singapore Mission. I observed two basic responses to more difficult cases, especially when out-of-the-ordinary mannerisms and behaviour were manifested. Some saw prayer for deliverance as the appropriate way forward. Others initiated counselling and therapy. Not only were these two basic responses true of the counsellors, they were also true of the more experienced supervisors.

Two possible mistakes

I believe we should avoid two mistakes in such situations. One is to literally, or de facto,[8] exclude the possibility of the demonic altogether. The other is to be too quick to assume the demonic as the cause and dismiss the possibility of psychosis.

Through deliverance, people who were unsuccessfully treated by counsellors, psychologists and psychiatrists have experienced healing. The reverse has also been true! Psychiatric treatment and psychotherapy have brought a real measure of healing to people who remained unwell or became worse following deliverance ministry. A Christian sister in the United Kingdom related her experience to me. Because of her depression she was taken to a home for deliverance. When she arrived she was ushered into the toilet, told to put her head over the toilet bowl and vomit out the 'spirit of depression'. She needed therapy to help her recover from the emotional and psychological trauma of that experience.

Behavioural and mental disorders may be due to the demonic or to mental illness or to a combination of both. I suspect that as mental and behavioural disorders increase in degree and intensity, there is a corresponding increase in the tendency for Christians to attribute such disorders to the demonic. Particularly, if they involve out-of-character bizarre behaviour such as hearing unwanted voices or struggling with obsessional thoughts which, while internal, seem alien. In these situations, it is not difficult to think one is possessed by an evil spirit. However, such phenomena can also be the symptoms of schizophrenia. The late Anthony Yeo said that any behavioural disorder which manifests itself in demon possession can also be symptoms of schizophrenia and other delusional disorders. I illustrate this in the diagram below which shows that any degree of disorder may be wholly demonic in origin (1), wholly mental illness (3) or a combination of both (2).

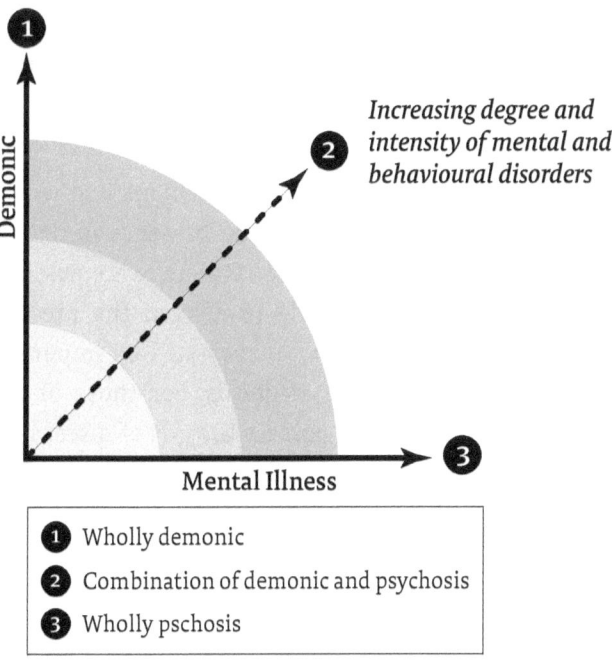

1. Wholly demonic
2. Combination of demonic and psychosis
3. Wholly pschosis

Mental Illness

Reaching a right diagnosis

It is important to reach a correct diagnosis and apply appropriate treatment. If a person's mental and behavioural disorders are wholly demonic in origin, counselling and medication without deliverance will not be effective. Conversely, if they are the symptoms of mental illness then deliverance ministry will neither be appropriate nor effective. Psychiatric treatment will be required.

It is important to reach a correct diagnosis and apply appropriate treatment.

How do we reach a correct diagnosis? Trained psychiatrists, psychologists and counsellors should be able to discern and diagnose mental illness. My psychiatrist, Dr Keith Chee, once commented that "there are some psychiatric syndromes which have a clear 'fingerprint' of features (signs and symptoms) which are characteristic, just as other medical syndromes like stomach ulcers or epilepsy have certain diagnostic characteristics".

Therapists who are also mature Christians and well-grounded in Scripture may be able to discern the presence of demonism and distinguish it from mental illness. Others who possess the gift of discerning spirits may be able to discern the presence of the demonic. In both cases, however, it may still be important to take a case history to confirm the diagnosis. For those of us who are neither trained therapists nor possess the gift of discerning spirits, I commend the practice of taking a case history. This practice was introduced to me many years ago. I was counselling a recovering drug addict who was experiencing much struggle and resistance with basic Christian disciplines like prayer and Bible study. I walked him through various possible reasons for this but none seemed to apply. He mentioned he was about to be baptised. I knew that many non-Christian families considered baptism the point of no return. I began to wonder whether his struggle with prayer and Bible study was the last ditch effort of the demonic to sway him from baptism.

These days, when people talk about experiencing occult phenomena I ask them whether they have been offered to, or been adopted by, a temple deity and whether they have been dabbling with the occult. But at the time, I had almost no experience of things occult and demonic. I phoned Reverend Philip Heng who was involved in a ministry of exorcism. I took the young man to see him. I half expected Reverend Heng to begin some ritual of exorcism. Instead he invited the young man to sit down, got out notepaper and a pen and began to take a case history. After clarifying the young man's current struggles

Reverend Heng asked about his family background and upbringing. Did he or his family have dealings with the occult or the temple? Had he experienced big disappointments in his life, broken relationships, failures? What happened that evening made a great impression upon me. It is now part of my standard practice in such situations to take a case history. The more that case history involves things occult and temple the more likely the cause is demonic. If things occult and temple are absent but emotional traumas, failures and disappointments in life have occurred, the more likely the disorders are due to mental illness.

I mentioned above that Christians tend to respond in one of two ways when faced with mental and behavioural disorders. Some are more predisposed to see the demonic at work. Others are more predisposed towards a medical-psychological explanation. Here we tend to be influenced by our training and our Christian upbringing. Those in more charismatic circles are generally more ready to attribute such disorders to the demonic. Others, say from a more reformed background, will tend to see a medical-psychological explanation. We all need to be self-aware. We are blessed if we are humbly open to various possibilities, even possibilities with which we have less affinity.

 ## Melody's Experience

Not demonism[9]

I have been through some 'exorcisms' before, where a pastor of a small charismatic church spent several sessions yelling at the demonic presence in me. I guess it appeared demonic because of what my doctor called 'insiders'. I had entities that were very much alive to me. Medical literature has fancier names for them — dissociative identity disorder or multiple personality disorder. My doctor never felt they were of no use in my illness. These entities expressed my fractured emotions which I, in turn, was not able to freely express. Dr Nelson always asked me how my 'insiders' were. He knew they accurately expressed my true feelings, when my veneer could not. Sometimes I would take the role of each of them, to show him my subconscious thoughts. I am told by many that I am intelligent. I see this mechanism of coping as my intelligent way of dealing with torrents of emotion and as a tool to keep me under control. They are neither demonic nor dangerous. They are parts of me that I was too afraid to reveal.

Anti-anxiety medication

I am taking anti-anxiety medication because of the conditioning I experienced in my early life. I was told repeatedly by my late grandma that my mom will hit and kill me. I thus lived in fear of her and even my mom's perfume would make my heart race. Also, when my mom disciplined me, she occasionally expressed it physically and that made me fear and dread her a lot. At age seven I really needed a parent's approval because my dad, whom I loved much, had left us for another woman. My mom was in grief herself over her failed marriage and so her expressions of love were erratic. I felt hated and this was reinforced by my mom's accusation that I was the third girl of three daughters. According to her, my father wanted a male child and the disappointment caused the breakdown of the marriage. As such, my anxiety is not caused by a lack of restfulness in Christ, but is more of a physical-psychological-sensorial experience that had its roots in the circumstances surrounding my upbringing.

Breakthrough

My breakthrough started when I allowed the past that took my present hostage to be resolved within me. The turbulence within me was due to my unfulfilled longing for love and attention from an absent caregiver father figure. Ever since my childhood, I had filled my empty love tank with affection from others. Now, I found my love tank filled by the 'love messages' found in the Bible, the close attention provided by the Holy Spirit and the prayers of many who cared. My life took a turn for the better when I forgave my mom and showed her love. I also chose to see her differently — as a wounded person rather than a menacing figure. I am of age to marry and I can see how my dad had fallen into adultery because his marriage did not fulfil him. As such, I forgave him who is but mortal. Forgiveness and total surrender of my life to Christ made my depression easier to handle, and my errant thoughts easier to rein in.

Synergy

This breakthrough went hand in hand with medication and therapy. Prior to going on medication, I suffered a lot from depression, anxiety and mood swings.

Working closely with my psychiatrist, I tried many kinds of medication before settling on a right combination that helped to keep me well. The synergy of right medication and making a conscious choice to think about my life differently has made me a healthier person mentally. Currently, I am on four medicines which work for me — antidepressant, anti-psychotic, mood stabiliser and anti-anxiety. These are the mainstay for my diagnosis — bipolar mood disorder. Without this medication, I would be so sick, so messed up in my head, so suicidal that I would be inconsolable, unable to be helped by anyone or anything, not even Scripture. In such a state, I often ended up in a psychiatric ward for my own safety.

Empowered with good mental health and a strong dependence on God, I am now able to earn a comfortable income and be effective in my vocation. This is something that, during my sickest moments, I never thought would be possible.

Meaningful hymn

I end this testimony with a hymn that speaks right to the point of the mind-transformation that has made my life so much more liveable.

May the Mind of Christ, My Savior

May the mind of Christ, my Savior,
Live in me from day to day,
By His love and power controlling
All I do and say.

May the Word of God dwell richly
In my heart from hour to hour,
So that all may see I triumph
Only through His power.

May the peace of God my Father
Rule my life in everything,
That I may be calm to comfort
Sick and sorrowing.

May the love of Jesus fill me
As the waters fill the sea;
Him exalting, self abasing,
This is victory.

May I run the race before me,
Strong and brave to face the foe,
Looking only unto Jesus
As I onward go.

May His beauty rest upon me,
As I seek the lost to win,
And may they forget the channel,
Seeing only Him.

Further Reading

Rita Goh, *Back from the Brink of Insanity* (Singapore: Rita Goh, 2005).

Harris Ng, *Recovered Grace: Schizophrenia* (Singapore: Harris Ng, 2005).

NHG Psychiatry Workgroup, *A Patient Education Guide to Living with Psychosis* (Singapore: National Healthcare Group, n.d.).

NHG Psychiatry Workgroup, *A Patient Education Guide to Living with Schizophrenia* (Singapore: National Healthcare Group, n.d.).

Robert Solomon, *Living in Two Worlds: Pastoral Responses to Possession in Singapore* (Frankfurt, Germany: Peter Lang International Academic Publishers, 1994).

Mood Disorders

Myths and Misconceptions

When it comes to mood disorders like depression, many people, including Christians, have various myths and misconceptions. There are Christians who do not want to take antidepressants because they are afraid of becoming addicted. The modern generation of antidepressants are not addictive. Others have the nagging thought they should be praying and exercising faith for healing rather than relying on antidepressants. This thinking is quite prevalent in some Christian circles. A member of my Singapore church twice started a course of antidepressants without completing it because she felt she should be trusting God for healing, not antidepressants. One Sunday morning she heard me share from the pulpit that I was on an antidepressant and would probably be on it for the rest of my life. For the first time she completed her full course of antidepressant and consequently got better. Her psychiatrist told her of another patient of his whose pastor had thrown her antidepressants away saying she needed to trust God for healing, not antidepressants. A little later she jumped! That pastor's intention may have been good but not his theology! Faith and medication are normally allies not enemies. Of course, God may choose to heal miraculously in answer to faith and prayer.[10] He also heals through medication and therapy.

Then there are those who are quick to tell a depressed person to snap out of it. However, if this is all that is needed for me to get out of my depression don't you think I would have done so? Do I want to remain and wallow in my depression? Depression is an unwanted illness. It is debilitating for it affects a person mentally, emotionally and bodily.[11]

Depression affects mind and body

Mental abilities
Trouble remembering, concentrating, deciding and negative thoughts.

Emotions
May feel miserable, distressed and helpless. Do not experience pleasure even in pleasurable situations.

Body
Disturbed sleep. Aches and pains. Fast heart beat. Changed appetite. Loss of sexual desire.

If only the answer to all this was as easy as just snapping out of it!

Others say depression is all in the mind. Just straighten out your thinking, become more positive and the depression will go away. I heard a person scold his brother along these lines, "You're always a loser. You cop out too easily! There's no reason for you to be depressed. There are millions of people worse off than you. Think how fortunate you are and snap out of it." But the negative, pessimistic thinking is more a symptom of depression than a cause. It is generally thought that depression is linked to a biochemical imbalance in the neurotransmitter serotonin located in the middle part of the brain that controls moods.

If a person is suffering an asthmatic attack do we say, "Look, it's all in your mind, just straighten out your thinking and the asthmatic attack will go away"? If he reached for his Ventolin inhaler would we say, "You should be trusting God for healing instead of relying on the Ventolin"? I do not think we would. Yet many would say such things to a person in depression! Why? What is the difference? Both are illnesses with medical causes. Both are caused by a dysfunction in our bodily system – asthma by constriction of the bronchial tubes and depression by a biochemical imbalance in the middle brain. Medication in both cases seeks to deal with the dysfunction so as to restore normal functioning and wellness.

What does the Bible say about depression? The following are two sermons of mine (revised and updated). The first is on Jeremiah and Elijah and their experience of depression and healing. The second is on Psalms 42 and 43 which give us insights into a Temple singer/helper who wrestled with his depression. The two sermons are followed by an article where I share my own journey with depression and a testimony by Ng Bee Ying, a former policewoman and then full-time church staff who struggled for years with severe depression.

 ## Jeremiah, Elijah and Depression
A sermon based on 1 Kings 19 and Jeremiah 20.7–18

The prophet Jeremiah wanted to give up. "Cursed be the day I was born! May the day my mother bore me *not* be blessed...Why did I ever come out of the womb to see trouble and sorrow and to end my days in shame?" (Jeremiah 20.14, 18; emphasis mine) This also happened to the prophet Elijah who had been such a faithful, bold servant of the Lord. Remember how he defied King Ahab and Queen Jezebel? Single-handedly he confronted the 850 false prophets of Baal and Asherah on Mount Carmel and won a great victory over them (1 Kings 18.16–40).

On Mount Carmel, Elijah had a literal and spiritual mountain-top experience! He would have been elated emotionally and morale-wise. Yet just a day or two later he wanted to end his life! 1 Kings 19.4b records this for us: "He came to a broom tree, sat down under it and prayed that he might die. 'I have had enough, LORD...Take my life; I am no better than my ancestors.'" Elijah was a great man of God, a spiritual giant! Yet he now wanted to die! Through God's power, he had experienced a tremendous victory but now he felt an abject failure! What was it that brought Elijah from elation to despair? Why did spiritual giants like Jeremiah and Elijah want to end their lives? Let me share with you three reasons I see in Jeremiah and Elijah's situations!

Opposition and rejection

Why was Jeremiah so discouraged that he wanted to die? It was the opposition, rejection, ridicule and mocking! "I am ridiculed all day long; everyone mocks me...the word of the LORD has brought me insult and reproach all day long...I hear many whispering, 'Terror on every side! Report him! Let's report him!'" (Jeremiah 20.7–10). Such opposition and rejection proved too much for Jeremiah.

For a brief moment, Jeremiah's spirit seemed to rally (20.11–12).

> But the LORD is with me like a mighty warrior; so my persecutors will stumble and not prevail. They will fail and be thoroughly disgraced; their dishonour will never be forgotten. O LORD Almighty, you who examine the righteous and probe the heart and mind, let me see your vengeance upon them, for to you I have committed my cause.

However, he soon lapsed back into his depression, "Cursed be the day I was born!" (20.14). Even his friends had turned against him because of the message of judgement and doom which God had commanded him to proclaim to his own people, "All my friends are waiting for me to slip, saying, 'Perhaps he will be deceived; then we will prevail over him and take our revenge on him.'" (20.10b). Opposition, ridicule and rejection from critics and enemies are difficult enough to cope with but when they come from one's friends, it can be too much.

> Opposition, ridicule and rejection from critics and enemies are difficult enough to cope with but when they come from one's friends, it can be too much.

Opposition was also a main cause for Elijah's depression,

> Now Ahab told Jezebel everything Elijah had done and how he had killed all the prophets with the sword. So Jezebel sent a messenger to Elijah to say, 'May the gods deal with me, be it ever so severely, if by this time tomorrow I do not make your life like that of one of them.' (1 Kings 19.1–2)

Had Elijah anticipated Jezebel's vehement hostility? Probably not! After the fire from God had so dramatically consumed the water-drenched sacrifice, after the false priests and prophets had been routed and slain, and after the apparent submission of King Ahab, Elijah may have assumed victory was complete and there would be no more opposition. If so, he was mistaken. Jezebel was determined to take Elijah's life. Elijah's response was rather surprising – he fled! Elijah's failure to anticipate Jezebel's vehement hostility and the power of evil that lay behind it helps us understand his reaction. Dr Ronald Wallace has written,

> Elijah had underestimated the resilient power of evil. The evil forces around us against which we have to enter into

conflict when we are led by God's Spirit, have enormous resources. The apostle Paul warns that after we have defeated them we must expect immediate counter-attack. It will come with such force, moreover, that we will find it difficult 'to stand' against it unless we remain strong and watchful (Ephesians 6.13).[12]

It can be very discouraging when people oppose or reject us because they are convinced we are wrong and mistaken when we believe we are right. We may become so frustrated, disappointed, hurt, angry and discouraged that we are sorely tempted to give up and leave the ministry. There was a period while ministering in Sydney when I faced serious misunderstanding and rejection. I wanted to quickly terminate my ministry there and hurry back to Singapore. But when I was in Singapore, I again experienced misunderstanding and rejection and wanted to return quickly to Sydney.[13] (How short my memory must have been!) Opposition and rejection can be a major cause of discouragement and depression. In Elijah's case, there were also other factors.

A sense of aloneness in the ministry

Listen to Elijah's complaint, "I have been very zealous for the LORD God Almighty. The Israelites have rejected your covenant, broken down your altars, and put your prophets to death with the sword. *'I am the only one left, and now they are trying to kill me too'*" (19.10; emphasis mine).

In 1981, I was Acting-Dean at the Discipleship Training Centre (DTC). I had a bad case of aloneness in ministry – not in the sense that I thought I was the only one in the right, but when I most needed understanding and support I felt I least received it. I was really struggling and not coping. Looking back, I now realise I was in depression, but at the time I was not aware of this. Others misunderstood and criticised me. What was worse, I felt my colleagues were not supportive. Instead they also seemed to be critical of me. As a result, I felt so alone in my struggling. This really ate away at my zeal to serve the Lord, especially my zeal to serve others. So for the first time in seven years I consciously and deliberately shut the door to my office to keep people out! On another occasion, while still at DTC, I felt as if I was drowning — it was an awful feeling. I felt so alone at a time when I most needed encouragement and support! This sense of aloneness can result in great discouragement and trigger depression.

Physical exhaustion

On Mount Carmel, Elijah had single-handedly fought a fierce, intense spiritual battle. After this spiritual battle which must have drained away much of his physical and emotional energy, Elijah ran all the way to Jezreel 50 kilometres away. In Jezreel, he learned of Jezebel's vow to kill him so he fled to Beersheba a further 150 kilometres away. From there he went another full day's journey into the desert! Where did Elijah find the strength and stamina to do all this? He must have been physically and emotionally exhausted. No doubt this contributed to his depression and desire to end his life. We should not underestimate the part physical tiredness and ill-health play in depression. I mentioned earlier that some time ago I felt as if I was drowning. I came to understand this was partly due to my physical and emotional tiredness. I was suffering from a bad case of jetlag. I had too much to do. I was stressed, discouraged and losing it.

How are we to cope with discouragement and depression?

In various circumstances, it is quite normal for Christians to become discouraged. Even depression may sometimes be a normal healthy reaction. Some Christians are too quick to condemn other Christians who experience depression. They think Christians should always be rejoicing and victorious and that depression is incompatible with rejoicing. It is true that Philippians 4.4 exhorts Christians to "Rejoice in the Lord always"! But this does not mean Christians can never question or doubt or experience depression. I believe even committed Christians may become clinically depressed. When depressed, I may not readily lift my voice in joyful praise and worship nor often experience feelings of happiness and joy but I do experience peace, contentment and thankfulness to the Lord for His grace to me and through me.

I have inherited a biochemical predisposition towards depression which can be triggered by work-related stress, together with unsympathetic, harsh criticism of my ministry. I believe the Lord is understanding and does not condemn us when we have doubts or are discouraged or become depressed. At the same time the Lord does not want us to remain discouraged or depressed.

How did God deal with Elijah's discouragement and depression? What was the very first thing that happened to Elijah after he voiced his desire to die? There are those who would move straight into a prayer and deliverance ministry.[14] In some cases this might be appropriate. But what happened with Elijah? "Then he lay down under the tree and fell asleep" (19.5a)! The Lord let him sleep. Not very dramatic, was it? Almost an anticlimax! But that was what Elijah needed and that was what the Lord provided. What was the next thing the Lord did for Elijah? "All at once an angel touched him and said, 'Get up...'" What for? "'Get up and eat.' He looked around and there by his head was a cake of bread baked over hot coals, and a jar of water. He ate and drank and then lay down again" (19.5b–6). The Lord knew Elijah's priority need at that moment was for physical sustenance and further rest. So He provided it! We must not neglect our physical needs. We need proper rest, recreation and a healthy diet. When we are physically healthy we are more resistant, not only to physical illness, but also to discouragement and depression.

After this, God had Elijah journey to Horeb for God would appear to him there and speak to him as He had earlier spoken to Moses. The Lord spoke to Elijah in a gentle whisper...Elijah heard and responded (19.12–13)! We, however, are often so busy, hassled and caught up with too much activity and noise that we fail to hear the Lord. We need to seek the Lord's presence and be still so that even if the Lord should speak to us in a gentle whisper we will hear Him. Spending adequate time in the Lord's presence listening to Him and communing with Him must always be a non-negotiable first priority for every Christian. The more we look after our physical and spiritual health, the more we will get things into right focus.

Our sense of aloneness or our belief that others are critical of us may be self-perception, not objective reality. When we are overtired and stressed and not walking well with the Lord, we can become oversensitive, even paranoid. When we become rightly focused we will become less paranoid. We will realise we are not alone. There are others on our side. God informed Elijah there were still seven thousand in Israel who were faithful to the Lord. Elijah wasn't the only one left (19.18). Very rarely, will we be on our own. Let's get things in proper focus and see things from God's perspective. We will only be able to do this when we spend adequate time with Him.

> The more we look after our physical and spiritual health the more we will get things into right focus.

Finally, God entrusted Elijah with a series of important tasks (19.15–17). Elijah was still useful in God's service. Note that the nature of the tasks shows it was God who determined the course of events, not Jezebel!

Let me conclude with an extended extract from Roy Clements,[15] which I personally found very encouraging:

> But it is generally accepted today that the roots of some sorts of depression are organic. Some of us, it seems, are naturally

more inclined to feel down in the dumps than others...A melancholy temperament is something that some of us are stuck with...We have to learn to cope with it...Some Christians are melancholics just as there are non-Christian melancholics and both have a tendency to get depressed. Indeed many of the great saints that we meet, both in the Bible and down through Christian history have had a melancholic trait to their personality. Take prophets like Jeremiah or Elijah; think of poets like William Cowper who wrote hymns that are sung today; even CH Spurgeon the great Baptist preacher. It is no denigration of the spirituality of these men that they knew unhappy moods. On the contrary, it is a tribute to their spirituality that in spite of such spiritual handicaps, they nevertheless achieved so much. I suspect some of them in fact would have testified that the unusual intimacy of their personal walk with God was in some measure the result of the temperament which God, in his providence, had assigned to them. Depression is not necessarily a sign of spiritual weakness. It can be an opportunity for extraordinary spiritual growth.

Why are You Downcast, O My Soul?
A meditation on Psalms 42 and 43[16]

Spiritual dryness

The Psalmist, a Temple musician and singer, was prevented by circumstances from returning to the Temple in Jerusalem. Separated from the worship and presence of God at the Temple, he experienced increasing spiritual emptiness and dryness: "As the deer pants for streams of water, so my soul pants for you, O God. My soul thirsts for God, for the living God. When can I go and meet with God?" (Psalm 42.1–2).

Have you also had this experience? The experience of being away from God and yet longing desperately after Him? I have, during a severe spiritual drought in my earlier years as a Christian. It began with a growing spiritual dryness and lasted for eight months. Prayer had become a meaningless ritual because my prayers seemed to bounce back from the ceiling. I derived little from my daily study of the Bible and constantly struggled with wandering thoughts. I could no longer experience the presence of the Lord. I longed for His presence but He seemed to have gone into hiding! As leader of the Youth Fellowship I had to keep going as an active Christian leader despite my spiritual dryness. Thankfully, God placed in me a deep thirsting after Him. Early each morning I continued to seek Him, sometimes waking about 5.00 a.m. I would kneel before the open window of my bedroom with the cold air coming in or even kneel outside in winter on the tiled verandah of our house.

It was mid-winter when I came to Psalms 42–43. The Psalmist's words found an echo in my heart, "As the deer pants for streams of water, so my soul pants for you, O God. My soul thirsts for God, for the living God. When can I go and meet with God?" My tears flowed when I came to verse 3, "My tears have been my food day and night". Like the Psalmist in verse 4, I too remembered the former days when "I used to go with the multitude, leading the procession to the house of God, with shouts of joy and thanksgiving among the festive throng". However, that was before, and now it was "Why are you downcast, O my soul? Why so disturbed within me?" (5). As soon as the Psalmist had expressed these sentiments, he immediately exhorted himself to snap out of it: "Put your hope in God, for I will yet praise him, my Savior and my God" (5-6).

The psalmist's faith wrestled with his depression

Spurgeon commented,

> As though he were two men, the Psalmist talks to himself. His faith reasons with his fears. His hopes argue with his sorrows. These present troubles, are they to last forever? The rejoicings of my foes, are they more than empty talk? My absence from the solemn feasts, is that a perpetual exile? Why this deep depression, this faithless fainting...?

Right throughout these two Psalms, we see this dialogue between faith and depression or perhaps more aptly, this struggle, this wrestling between faith and depression. Each doubt or question was immediately followed by an affirmation of faith and hope. However, as soon as the affirmation had been made, he was down again. "My soul is downcast within me" (6)! But rather than succumb to this downward pull, the Psalmist resolved to fight it. I might have expected him to say, "My soul is downcast within me therefore I want to give up"! Instead, he exclaimed, "My soul is downcast...therefore I will remember you". Even though it can be so hard to determine to remember the Lord when one is feeling very down, the Psalmist knew that if he did not do so, he would be in grave spiritual danger!

When doubt and depression threaten to overcome us, it is difficult to be positive and objective. The Psalmist (6b) deliberately cast his mind away from his doubts and recalled happier days with the Lord. The times of sweet refreshing communion with the Lord by the banks of the Jordan or on the heights of Hermon or the slopes of Mount Mizar...But the next moment he was down again, almost overwhelmed by his depression, "Deep calls to deep in the roar of your waterfalls; all your waves and breakers have swept over me..." (7). The Psalmist's thoughts were in turmoil as he saw the waters of the Jordan cascading over the boulders and rocks. He pictured himself overwhelmed by these waters, his footing gone and wave after wave sweeping over him. Yet even here faith asserted itself, for the waterfalls were still God's waterfalls and the waves and breakers were God's waves and breakers. He recognised that even the most overwhelming of circumstances had been allowed by God. God had not lost control. He was still sovereign.

His faith rose to the fore in verse 8: "By day the LORD directs his love"! Though the Lord seemed far off and his thoughts were frequently in turmoil and he often felt overwhelmed, the Psalmist nevertheless trusted that God still loved him. In the darkness of the night the Lord's song remained present with him. Even in the overwhelming floods, he did not let go. But he did question. He did doubt. He didn't just hang on stoically, passively, silently. He wanted answers: "I say to God my Rock (*God was still his Rock, his security!*), 'Why have you forgotten me? Why must I go about mourning, oppressed by the enemy?'" (9). Questions and doubts are not necessarily inconsistent with faith. To question is not necessarily a sign of lack of faith. Sometimes such struggles indicate that faith is still alive! I think of salmon which swim upstream against the flow in order to reach the head of the river to spawn. That these salmon struggle is a sign of life. The ones that do not struggle are those that have reached the head of the river or those which are dead!

Psalm 43 begins on a more positive note. There are still the ups and downs but there is now a more positive spirit of hope! For example verses 1 and 3, and in particular, verse 4, "Then I will go to the altar of God, to God, my joy and my delight. I will praise you with the harp, O God, my God"! At this point the Psalmist was not talking about a literal return to the Temple in Jerusalem. He had reached the point when he knew the presence of God could be found wherever he was, even when far away from the Temple. He now knew he could praise and worship God in faith wherever and whatever the circumstances. This was indeed a deliverance, a victory for him.

> To question is not necessarily a sign of lack of faith.

One of the greatest blessings I received from my eight months of spiritual drought was learning to hang on to the Lord and to trust Him even in the midst of a spiritual depression, with my prayers bouncing back from the ceiling, getting little from my daily Bible study, my spirit dry and empty, and God seemingly in hiding.

It was near the end of that period of drought and depression that I read the familiar words of Habakkuk 3.17–19, "Though the fig tree does not bud and there are no grapes on the vines, though the olive crop fails and the fields produce no food, though there are no sheep in the pen and no cattle in the stalls (*what a picture of utter desolation and void*), yet I will rejoice in the LORD, I will be joyful in God my Savior"!

When I read these words, I wept. I can still picture the scene fifty years ago, sitting on the front lawn of Sydney University on a winter's night. I wept for I knew then what the Lord had been doing in my life. He had been teaching me to trust Him even when everything seemed so dry and empty. I thank the Lord for that precious, invaluable lesson.

Looking back, I now realise my spiritual drought, my spiritual depression, was, in fact, clinical depression. But, since by God's grace, the Lord Jesus was the centre of my life, my clinical depression manifested itself spiritually with spiritual symptoms.

Five symptoms of depression

One Bible teacher has discerned five symptoms of depression in Psalms 42–43:[17]

1. *Crying*

    First of all, the Psalmist says he couldn't stop crying. "My tears have been my food day and night" (42.3). An inability to control one's emotions is a very common feature of depression. One feels weepy, often crying for no apparent reason.

2.   *Fatigue*

The Psalmist tells us he felt completely lacking in energy. 'Downcast' is the word he used repeatedly, "My soul is downcast within me" or literally "My soul prostrates itself". In contemporary idiom we might say he felt utterly 'flat'. There was no spark of enthusiasm for anything, just a kind of inner fatigue, a sagging of the spirit. Depressed people often complain of being permanently tired.

3.   *Emotional disturbance*

He also says he felt a continual emotional upheaval going on inside him. "Why are you so disturbed within me, my soul?"

4.   *Feeling overwhelmed*

Furthermore, he felt utterly overwhelmed: "Deep calls to deep in the roar of your waterfalls; all your waves and breakers have swept over me". Many depressed people use similar metaphors. Often they will talk about being 'drowned' by circumstances, 'everything is on top of them'. I recall a cousin of mine telling me he felt he was drowning, finding it hard to keep his head above water. The next morning his brother came across his body in the kitchen. He had gassed himself.

5.   *Feelings of rejection*

Perhaps most characteristic of all was the language the Psalmist used to describe deprivation of affection and bereavement. "Why have you forgotten me? Why have you rejected me? I go about mourning because of the enemy" (42.9; 43.2). His whole personality was torn by a sense of loss. Depression is often associated with such feelings. Clements writes,

Like so many Christians in such a situation, the inspired poet finds himself bewildered and frustrated because he can perceive the incongruity, the inappropriateness of feeling like that. 'I am a believer,' he says, 'I shouldn't feel like this. Why am I so downcast? Why so inwardly disturbed? What has happened to me? What has happened to my faith?' It is natural to ask such questions like that. Though we may think we ought not to feel like this, there is no necessary criticism, no necessary disparagement, no necessary condemnation of our spiritual lives in such an experience. Indeed, in my judgement, the very way this man wrestles with his rebel emotions...bears testimony not to the weakness of his faith at all, but to the extraordinary vitality and tenacity of it. You don't come away from this Psalm thinking to yourself, what a spiritual wimp that fellow was! Instead you come away just a little bit envious of him!

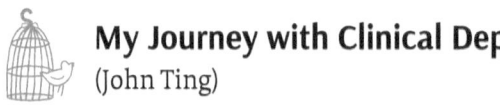

My Journey with Clinical Depression
(John Ting)

Diagnosed with clinical depression

In October 1996, during morning quiet time, I was feeling rather melancholic. Things had not been going well and I began to understand both emotionally and cognitively why people thought of ending their life! What had brought me to this point? I had reacted more than I realised to Dad's passing away a few months earlier. I thought I had coped quite well but apparently this was not so. Furthermore, I was losing my grip on things. Various matters seemed to be spinning out of my control. Dad had looked after various aspects of our family financial affairs. Taking back this responsibility together with moving Mum from hospital to nursing home and now shouldering her financial affairs proved too much when added to my family and church responsibilities. At the time, I was also experiencing tension with some of the leadership at church. It seemed my integrity was being questioned and I felt shackled in my ministry. Frances was visiting her family in Hong Kong so I felt rather alone as I struggled with all these matters. Thankfully, the empathy I felt that morning in 1996 for those who contemplated suicide, never returned. But I continued to have difficulty coping.

Three years later in 1999, some friends joined us for dinner. 'Sonia' talked freely about her depression. She mentioned that during her depression she had been unable to do even normal tasks like cooking. I began to wonder whether certain behaviours of mine which I had always attributed to undue stress were actually symptoms of depression. So I went to see a psychiatrist. In April 1999 I was put on antidepressant medication and, initially, remained on it for twenty months.[18] Dr Keith Chee, a good consultant psychiatrist and committed Christian, had diagnosed that I was clinically depressed.

At my first session, I mentioned my mother's post-natal depression. Dr Chee thought I had very likely inherited from my mother a biochemical predisposition towards depression which could be triggered by various factors. I also had other symptoms. I was constantly frustrated by my lack of productivity. Being unsettled for most of the day, I could not handle more than a couple of strands of work at any one time. At the end of the day I often felt guilty and frustrated about all the wasted hours. This was my constant complaint in the five years or more of my time teaching at the Discipleship Training Centre up till the end of 1991. At best, I was operating at only 70 percent of my capacity. This continued on and off in my years back in Sydney from 1992 until 1999 when I started on antidepressant medication. I had poor sleeping habits, often waking in the early morning. I felt constantly weary and emotionally and physically fatigued. I was tense, irritable, overly critical and easily disturbed and 'jarred' by noise.

Perhaps the most debilitating symptom was my pathological procrastination. The more my work load increased the more time I spent in front of the TV. I seemed to be paralysed. It became a vicious cycle. The more paralysed, the higher the work pile. The higher the work pile, the greater my paralysis and escapist activities. The worst period was probably in 1983 in the United Kingdom during a short sabbatical. My pathological procrastination, exacerbated by guilt and anxiety, was so bad it sometimes took me up to a week to open up a letter!

Now I realise I was suffering from depression at the time. I thank the Lord that during that sabbatical I also experienced deep healing without medication through wonderful extended times of quiet, prayer, fasting and reflection. In 1999–2000, the Lord healed me through medication. The medication helped greatly with my work productivity, irritability, sensitivity to noise, tendency to withdraw, perpetual weariness and procrastination. I was greatly encouraged to learn that CH Spurgeon, the great nineteenth-century preacher, suffered from depression. There was, and still is, hope for me!

Let's remove the stigma!

There are clinically depressed brothers and sisters in our churches who are active in some form of ministry. Most are afraid to let others know about it for fear of rejection and being judged untrusting and lacking in faith when this is probably not so.

Here is a letter slipped under the door of my room at a church camp in June 2001.

I was greatly encouraged to learn that CH Spurgeon, the great nineteenth-century preacher, suffered from depression.

Dear Rev Ting, about two months ago, my friend 'Mary' borrowed your sermon on 'Depression' for my viewing. Having suffered from depression since 1996, I am familiar with the many things you touched on in your sermon. I have tried several times to get off the medication without, so far, success. I have been told that my illness may be endogenous and that I may have to be on medication for the rest of my life. The reason why I am writing is because there is so much stigma attached to this illness in a place like Singapore that I would think a hundred times before sharing the problem with fellow Christians. I have been urged by Christian friends to 'get off the medication' or 'seek healing from God who is the ultimate healer Himself'. Even the general practitioner (a Christian) who I see advises me not to take the medication for too long. I am unable to share the blessings that I have experienced from God in coping with the illness or to ask for prayer in my struggles with my illness. It is my hope that respected and revered speakers like you would find opportunity to raise awareness and deepen the Christian community's understanding of this much misunderstood illness...

In Christ,
'Susan'

How does my depression affect my ministry?

My depression is like a handicap, a disability that limits my capacity to minister. In my case, depression causes inertia where I have little energy and motivation to get things done or to relate to people. Even relatively small things like phoning or emailing someone can be difficult to do. I have difficulty concentrating on more than one or two things at any one time. I am often tired physically and emotionally. Not surprisingly, I am not very productive. I become irritable and moody. Perhaps the worst symptom is my pathological procrastination. The larger the pile of work left undone, the more I procrastinate and the higher the pile grows!

I remember my first visit to Dr Chee. I said to him, "Maybe I should just accept these symptoms, these limitations as a part of me and learn to live with them. Maybe I should just accept that, at best, I am ever only going to operate at 70 percent of the efficiency/productivity that I am capable of, instead of being constantly frustrated and discouraged? Perhaps I should just accept my condition and learn to live with it. This way I may maximise the 70 percent. But If I keep on getting frustrated at not being able to achieve more than 70-percent productivity, I may not even reach 70 percent!"

How did Dr Chee respond? "Yes, what you have suggested is one way of coping. But what if medication can help you become over 90-percent productive and help you overcome your procrastination and weariness?"

My immediate response was, "Can medication really do this for me?!"

Antidepressant medication has helped greatly

Antidepressant medication has helped me greatly in overcoming my symptoms. My productivity quickly increased. I lost my weariness, became less irritable and did not procrastinate as much. The medication helped me so much that twenty months later, when Dr Chee said it was time to come off the medication, I was nervous about how I would cope without the medication. My wife and daughter expressed reservations about my readiness to come off! They had obviously benefited from my being on medication! The medication had facilitated my ministry. It had enabled me to work more productively, experience less tendency to withdraw and more feeling and passion in ministry. I was nicer when relating to others. Without the medication, I would have to work and struggle more in all these areas. Ministry would be less natural and less 'passion' driven.

At the Canberra Overseas Christian Fellowship Convention in 1998, I experienced something I had never experienced before. Despite spending much time in earnest prayer I felt completely 'flat' each time I went up to give the evening message. I was like a cola that had lost all its fizz! In my pastoral ministry, I experienced times when I had no motivation to make pastoral visits. Frances had to prompt and push me. Because there was little motivation or emotional drive I often had to 'will' myself to minister. This was what it was like during the periods when I was not on medication.

That was why I was nervous about coming off. However, if I want to finish well in my ministry, I have to accept that with my biochemical predisposition towards depression something of this may always be there. I need to understand that my working less productively, my tendency to withdraw, my possessing less passion and having to work more at ministry, are not necessarily due to less commitment or to backsliding but may be the symptoms of an unbalanced biochemistry!

Therefore, for me, ministry should mean faithfulness and perseverance both when I feel 'flat' and when I feel 'effervescent', when I feel little compassion and when I feel much, in periods when I struggle to get things done as well as when I am highly motivated and it comes easily. My biochemical predisposition also means I need to be more aware that undue work-related pressures can trigger off a relapse. In fact, I have not been sufficiently careful so I am presently back on antidepressant medication.

Certain parts of Scripture became more meaningful

Various Scripture passages have taken on added meaning for me:

> "For when I am weak, then I am strong." (2 Corinthians 12.10b)

> "I can do everything through him who gives me strength." (Philippians 4.13)

> "...in all these things we are more than conquerors through him who loved us..." (Romans 8.37)

> "During the days of Jesus' life on earth, he offered up prayers and petitions with loud cries and tears to the one who could save him from death..." (Hebrews 5.7a)

> "And, being in anguish, he prayed more earnestly, and his sweat was like drops of blood falling to the ground." (Luke 22.44)

The Lord Jesus may not have experienced clinical depression as we know it, but I believe He has experienced something of what depressed people experience and He understands.

Therefore, since we have a great high priest who has gone through the heavens, Jesus the Son of God, let us hold firmly to the faith we profess. For we do not have a high priest who is unable to sympathize with our weaknesses, but we have one who has been tempted in every way, just as we are — yet was without sin. Let us then approach the throne of grace with confidence, so that we may receive mercy and find grace to help us in our time of need. (Hebrews 4.14–16)

In Galatians 6.2 Paul exhorts us to "Carry each other's burdens and in this way you will fulfill the law of Christ". This surely includes bearing the burdens of those amongst us who experience depression!

 ## Ng Bee Ying: My Struggle with Severe Depression — Breaking Free of the Stigma

In 1992, without apparent reason, I sank into depression. I lost my appetite for food, could not concentrate and my mood plunged to rock bottom. I had little energy; even a simple task like shampooing my hair was a challenge. I slept a lot but was never refreshed. A sense of hopelessness and despair set in and I began to have suicidal thoughts. I could no longer pray as my mind was all 'knotted up' and my spirit was heavy. After several weeks, my sister-in-law advised me to see a psychiatrist. I knew I needed help.

Diagnosis
My friend drove me to the A&E Department of a local hospital to see the psychiatrist on duty. To assess my mental condition, he asked a simple multiplication question. I looked at him blankly and could not

give the answer. The doctor then prescribed me some antidepressants and gave me an appointment to see a consultant two weeks later.

The consultant diagnosed me as suffering from bipolar mood disorder or manic-depressive psychosis. In the manic stage, the sufferer feels 'high' with lots of energy to do various tasks and the mind remains alert and active through the night. Then the mood can plunge very low causing severe depression. For the first time then, I understood my medical condition. I realised that it was an illness that needed treatment. My battle of learning to cope with and fight this illness began.

After receiving my diagnosis, I tried to understand more about this condition. I learnt that any man or woman from any sector of the population could be hit by this disorder, which could be due to some chemical imbalance in the brain. If one member in the family had been diagnosed with a mental illness, chances would be higher for other family members to also suffer the same. My two elder sisters had been treated for schizophrenia and mood swings.

The consultant prescribed lithium a mood stabilizer and an antidepressant. Unfortunately, it did not help. I still suffered the erratic mood swings alternating between the highs and the lows. Most of the time I was in severe depression. Such moments were very painful and miserable. However, there were times when my mood went high, with thoughts racing day and night so that I could not sleep.

Help at last

After four years of regular consultation and medication, there was no improvement. My friend then came to know of the Clinic for Anxiety and Mood Disorder in another local hospital. She encouraged me to see a specialist. So in May 1996, we made our way to the hospital without any referral letter or prior appointment. There, I was fortunate to see a female psychiatrist who understood my condition after interviewing me. She put my heart at ease. Over the months of seeing her, I began to grow in confidence and trust her professional care and guidance. She was a good doctor who had genuine care and concern for her patients. She would discuss with me the medication available and prepare me for the side-effects. Such information was important because it prepared me psychologically to cope with the discomfort of adverse side effects. She was also easily available when I needed to consult her over the e-mail or telephone.

During an appointment with Dr Chan, she explained that depression was not an illness far worse than diabetes. Her rationale was if a diabetic person had to be treated to manage the disease, likewise a depressed person. With proper medication, a person with depressive illness would be able to live a normal life and excel like any person. That settled my doubt and apprehension.

However, my problems were made worse by the fact that due to my sensitive stomach, I could not tolerate the side effects of the medication. I experienced nausea, vomiting, bloated stomach and constipation. To date I have tried more than 13 different types of anti-depressants. Many medications were discontinued because either they were not suitable or I could not handle the side effects. If my stomach could talk, it would probably scream, "No more drugs!" Enormous weight gain also caused me to lay off some antidepressants.

On 15 August 1997, seeing no improvement, my psychiatrist suggested electro-convulsive therapy (ECT) as it would help to lift the mood faster than medication. I agreed as my suicidal tendencies were high and the pains of depression were overwhelming. She attended to me personally and I went through three ECTs under day care. The ECT did not wipe out my memory, contrary to my initial fear. It did, however, cause a momentary memory loss immediately after ECT. But by and by the memories returned.

Anguish

In the early stages of the illness, I could not understand why I was depressed as there was no apparent trigger. I could not accept leading such a defeated life, and felt ashamed to be depressed because it gave people the impression that I was weak emotionally, lacking in faith or not right in my Christian walk. I felt very guilty for sleeping too much when I was unwell. The depression shook my self-confidence and robbed me of the joy of living. What was worse, it had come upon me without warning. Up till then, I had been happily serving God in pastoral ministry. Oftentimes, I wished for death, as it would be the end of my suffering and misery.

In these moments of great mental suffering and pain, I told God that I was disappointed and angry with Him. In being truthful, I felt a release of my pent-up anger and frustration. The following verses in the Bible assured me that God understood my feeling:

> O LORD, you have searched me and you know me. You know when I sit and when I rise; you perceive my thoughts from afar. You discern my going out and my lying down; you are familiar with all my ways. Before a word is on my tongue you know it completely, O LORD. (Psalm 139:1–4)

There were times when I could not pray because my mood was very low and my mind could not concentrate. Many times I resorted to writing my prayers to God on pieces of paper. I have also shed enough tears over the past eleven years to form a mini swimming pool! On one occasion, too weak to pray, I sighed and whispered to God to please put me on some people's hearts to intercede on my behalf. Through the testimonies of brothers and sisters in the house group who shared of instances when they felt led to pray for me, I believe He answered even those whispered prayers. I thank God and those brethren who prayed for me in my moments of need.

Concerning the days ahead

It has been a long, arduous and difficult eleven years battling the illness. Many times I have felt as though I was in the wilderness alone; at the worst time there has been a strong temptation to jump from a high floor to end the pain. However, as I look back, I thank God for His keeping power and grace in my life. The thought of not causing further pain and sorrow to loved ones and the presence of good and supportive friends have also stopped me from resorting to such relief.

I live one day at a time, totally dependant on God's faithfulness and grace. My future is in His hands, knowing that He is always with me. In December 2001, I resigned from my position to seek God's new direction in my life. Now, despite having gone through many dark and gloomy days, I treasure every new day when I am healthy and happy. I have also gained the privilege and joy of being able to serve the Lord in lay capacity whenever my health enables me.

Though painful, I can continue this journey triumphantly because of God's promise in 2 Corinthians 2:14: "But thanks be to God, who always leads us in His triumph in Christ, and manifests through us the sweet aroma of the knowledge of Him in every place".

Ng Bee Ying worked as a policewoman for twelve years. In 1983, she resigned to answer God's call to work as a pastoral staff member in a local church. Presently, Bee Ying serves in the church in lay capacity.

Suicide

Can a true Christian commit suicide?

I think many Christians find it difficult to believe a committed Christian who is sincerely trying to trust God can commit suicide. For these Christians, the fact that a person committed suicide reveals he or she did not have a strong enough faith and trust in God. Others look upon suicide as one of the most grievous of sins – the taking of life, albeit one's own life. A related question is what kind of burial should they receive since they have committed a serious sin in taking their own lives? A factor for some Christians is that the person who commits suicide has sinned grievously without the opportunity to repent. Those from a Roman Catholic background may ask whether suicide is a mortal sin and therefore unforgivable.

I believe even true born-again Christians can commit suicide and they will go to heaven. A friend and former pastoral colleague who himself has had bouts of serious depression speaks of suicide as 'terminal spiritual cancer'. As a result of severe depression arising from a serious dysfunction in a person's brain system – a biochemical imbalance in the middle brain – a true Christian may end up taking his or her own life. Being a true Christian does not exempt him or her from diseases and illnesses such as terminal heart failure or terminal diabetes or terminal breast cancer. Neither does it exempt us from illnesses like bipolar condition or severe 'terminal' depression following serious dysfunction in a person's brain system.

At the same time, the spiritual resources available to Christians may help to lessen the incidence of suicide. My psychiatrist, Dr Keith Chee, commented to me, "I have found that the Christian perspective of truly surrendering to God's will, rather than controlling one's life and taking matters into one's own hands, gives much strength and protects against suicide."

 David's Case

David, a member of the young adults' group in my Sydney Church, suffered from bipolar illness for nearly twenty years. In his manic phases he made some very foolish decisions that brought him considerable financial and material loss. His depressive phases could be severe. One day his aged father discovered his forty-year-old son David hanging from the ceiling in his room. I was asked to conduct the funeral service and burial. What form should the funeral service take?

I did not know David well but on the few occasions I related to him, I had the impression that his Christian walk was real and he knew the Lord Jesus personally. I spoke to some of the leaders of the young adults' group and they had no doubts that David was a real Christian. On that basis I conducted a Christian funeral and burial.

But what about the fact that he had no opportunity to repent of his 'grievous' sin? Many of us know of people whom we believe were true, committed Christians who died suddenly, for example, in an accident. They would not have had an opportunity to repent of unconfessed sins. But most of us would be confident such a person would go to heaven, wouldn't we?

Further Reading

Roy Clements, *Songs of Experience* (Fearn, UK: Christian Focus, 1993).

Anxiety Disorders

Peace I leave with you; my peace I give you.
I do not give to you as the world gives.
Do not let your hearts be troubled and do not be afraid.
(John 14.27)

Jesus and Paul Taught Christians Not to Worry or Be Anxious

Jesus taught His followers not to worry about daily needs like food, drink and clothing because God knows and cares about these needs of ours and He is well able to provide. Thus Christians should not worry but should trust God and seek first His kingdom and His righteousness (Matthew 6.25–34). The apostle Paul wrote in Philippians 4.6–7, "Do not be anxious about anything, but in everything, by prayer and petition, with thanksgiving, present your requests to God. And the peace of God, which transcends all understanding, will guard your hearts and minds in Christ Jesus". The apostle Paul knew the reality of this in his own life:

> I have learned to be content whatever the circumstances. I
> know what it is to be in need, and I know what it is to have
> plenty. I have learned the secret of being content in any and
> every situation, whether well fed or hungry, whether living
> in plenty or in want. I can do everything through him who
> gives me strength. (Philippians 4.11–13)

We might think Paul could experience contentment and freedom
from anxiety because he was a spiritual giant. We are not in his league.
Yet we, more ordinary Christians, can also experience freedom from
anxiety when we have a right perspective of God's Fatherly care of us
and we are able to place our trust and rest in Him.

A Christian leader came to me weighed down and anxious
because he had committed sexual sin. He had not slept for nearly
a week. Having first ascertained his deep repentance, we turned to
Philippians 4.6–7, heeded its teaching and earnestly asked God to take
away the weight of guilt and anxiety and replace it with the peace
of God promised by the passage. The following day he smilingly and
excitedly told me he had slept for four hours or so! Another Christian
leader shared with me he was so anxious and weighed down by family
responsibilities and work pressure he had not been able to sleep for a
few days. I walked him through Philippians 4.6–7 and then we turned
the passage into heartfelt prayer. He telephoned me the next day to tell
me he had enjoyed some hours of sleep for the first time in days.

Countless Christians can testify to experiencing the deep peace
which only Jesus can give. For those who do not experience this peace
because they are weighed down by worry and anxiety, it is often because they have not heeded or not been able to respond to the invitation
of Jesus in Matthew 11.28–30,

> Come to me, all you who are weary and burdened, and I will
> give you rest. Take my yoke upon you and learn from me, for

I am gentle and humble in heart, and you will find rest for your souls. For my yoke is easy and my burden is light.

So, other things being equal, to be weighed down by worry and anxiety is not in line with the teachings of Jesus and Paul.

Does the Teaching of Jesus and Paul Apply to Anxiety Disorders?

Are anxiety disorders also not in line with the teachings of Jesus and Paul? Can true, committed Christians experience ongoing anxiety disorders? Yes, they can! I know of a Bible college student who experienced panic attacks caused by emotional trauma resulting from a 'roller-coaster' relationship. He experienced healing following appropriate counselling and medication. I do not think there was ever any question about his Christian commitment and practice of prayer during his period of depression and panic attacks.

Spiritual Resources Available to Christians can Help with Coping and Recovering better from Anxiety Disorders

Anxiety has a large cognitive component, so if a person has a strong biblical worldview, it can help him or her deal better with anxiety. A sound biblical worldview should include at least the following:

- A living trust in God's Fatherly concern and care for us (Matthew 6.26, 30, 32; 7.9–11);
- Being able to 'rest' in Jesus (Isaiah 30.15; Matthew 11.28–30)[19];

- God is a living God who intervenes on behalf of His children; He is a loving Father, not a demanding task-master (see pages 81 to 84 on justification by faith through grace, which I believe is very relevant); and
- A 'lively' belief that God is in sovereign control of our circumstances (Romans 8.28).

Some years ago, in Bangalore, India, I was discussing what is spirituality with a few of my former students. We began with an exercise — draw a symbol or picture which encapsulated our understanding of spirituality. For Peter it was a world full of faces and a hand over the world symbolising God's sovereign control over the affairs of the world in general and Peter's life in particular. This was such a living reality for Peter that he described his life as "like resting in a hammock"! Immediately I said to him, "So when that incident took place the hammock must have shaken and swayed!" (A couple of years earlier Peter had been kidnapped by Naga separatists and taken into the jungle at gunpoint!)

A strong and living faith in God's sovereignty can give Christians peace in place of fear and anxiety.

Peter replied, "No, as I went into the jungle I was very calm. I had no anxiety. I knew God was in control. In fact, during the few days in the jungle, I caught up on my sleep! I told the leader with the gun that I was not afraid to die because I knew Jesus."

Indeed a strong and living faith in God's sovereignty can give Christians peace in place of fear and anxiety. The more so if the particular anxiety disorder has a large cognitive, voluntary component. Where the anxiety disorder has a greater emotional, involuntary component such as post-traumatic stress disorder (PTSD), the less spiritual resources may help, at least until an adequate measure of healing has first taken place through therapy and medication.

A note of caution may be appropriate here. Crises and very difficult situations may not be appropriate times to seek to inculcate a biblical worldview. A person may not be able to 'hear' because he or she is too anxious and caught up with immediate concerns such as medical, housing, financial, physical, emotional, relational and mental ones.[20]

Nonetheless, answered prayers in crisis situations strengthen faith and reinforce in a practical way a biblical view of God. If we are able to walk alongside a person going through a crisis or experiencing great anxiety and stress, and if we are able to help him or her bring and yield that crisis or anxiety to the Lord in prayer, then if God were to unmistakably answer that prayer, the person's faith would be greatly strengthened. What might have been a merely theoretical, theological knowledge of God would become a practical, living reality.

What we need is wisdom and sensitivity to discern whether the presence of crisis, anxiety and stress means it is not an appropriate time to inculcate a biblical worldview or it is an opportunity to learn experientially God's sovereignty and faithfulness.

Moments of calm and stability are a good time to work at building a biblical worldview and growing in one's knowledge of God and His ways, so as to strengthen one's trust in Him. It is also an appropriate time to develop good support among fellow believers who can encourage and pray.[21]

 **Michael's Journey**[22]

Early symptoms

When I first experienced anxiety/panic attacks, I did not know what was happening to me. Thus I did not know where to seek help. I was generally known as a happy-go-lucky person, with a quirky sense of humour. So the feelings of anxiety and panic really caught me by surprise.

It started when I was beginning to commit to a new relationship. I was watching a movie with my girlfriend. After the movie, while we were having dinner, I felt breathlessness and numbness in my heart. I could not muster any feelings for my girlfriend and wondered why. It was emotionally very confusing and I was unable to relate properly to her.

A panic attack has been likened to being caught on a railway track with a train speeding towards us causing a surge of 'panicky feelings'. When I got home, these feelings did not stop. During the next few nights, in order to rid myself of the panic 'resting' on my chest, I repeatedly tried to vomit and spit out the unwanted feelings. By the end of the week, I was spitting out blood from a throat injured by too much coughing and vomiting.

Road to recovery

The road to recovery seemed long, but when I look back, I realise it was actually relatively short. God brought me out of the darkness by providing various people to show me different facets of my struggles, which I would not have seen if only one person had helped me.

Healing

The first person I spoke to about my anxiety disorder was my Christian mentor at my workplace. For over two years he had faithfully followed up with me on a weekly basis. When he heard my experience, he brought me to a church building near our office to pray. He prayed for me in tongues, while I was struggling with my panic attacks. Then my mentor tried to go through with me the *Steps to Freedom in Christ* workbook by Neil T Anderson. When I read the following words from the booklet, "You shall have no other gods before me" (Deuteronomy 6.7), I was struck with a sense of awe and conviction of my sins.

I started to weep. It brought to my mind an incident a few years before, when I still wasn't a Christian. I had bought a new robe for a Buddhist nun in South Korea. On this robe I had sewn my name, thinking that it would bring good "karma" to my life whenever the nun bowed and prayed to her gods. When I was working through *Steps* and renouncing my past, I was gripped by fear that my name still belonged to the 'gods' the nun had been praying to. I could sense a devilish darkness and ferocious anger from the forces that tried to cling on to my name. All this took place in broad daylight. I felt imprisoned and screamed out in both pain and fear, "Give me back my name! Give me back my name!" At that point, it dawned on me that I had been deceived and given over to the forces of darkness.

But just at this point of desperation, I sensed a deep sorrow and love for me and I realised that Jesus had broken into this darkness and was showing me He loved me even more than I could love myself. Wrapped in this love, my fears went away that very moment. I knew in my heart that Jesus had rescued me and my name was safely protected in His hands. That evening, my mentor brought me to his pastor, and we continued to work out the list of sins to confess. After the evening of prayer, I went home feeling much better. However, the anxiety attacks returned a few days later.

Subsequently, I signed up for a seminar conducted by a Christian ministry which focused on spiritual healing. However, although I greatly benefited from the 'spiritual healing' sessions, the teaching caused me to focus only on my sins. I became a kind of 'spiritual hypochondriac', always questioning whether there were still unconfessed sins which lay behind the recurrence of the panic attacks. Obviously, there was something lacking in the treatment.

Medication

Later on, I spoke with one of my church's younger pastors and he rightly pointed out to me that the symptoms I felt were signs of a panic attack. He shared about his own struggles with anxiety attacks in the past, and how medication had helped him overcome the issue. So taking his advice, I was linked up with a church member who was a psychiatrist. After diagnosis he prescribed Xanax, a medication that treats anxiety disorders. The receipt and prescription were labelled "Institute of Mental Health" so I did not dare claim medical expenses from my employer, fearing repercussions on my career development. When I presented the prescription at the pharmacy, I sensed cautious, unfriendly looks from behind the counter. The social stigma made my suffering worse. I dared not inform my immediate family. As I was still living with my parents, I had to take the medication secretly lest they came to know.

At this stage, the attacks were triggered when I found myself attracted to other girls, as I began to find my then girlfriend less and less attractive. I thought my panic attacks were due to commitment phobia (unable to commit to a relationship) caused by my previous bondage to pornography. Yet there were times when my girlfriend and I focused on Christ in our conversations and mutual encouragement and the fears subsided. These times were made possible by medication which reduced the intensity of the anxiety. I was able to renew my mind by focusing on whatever was true, noble, right, pure, lovely and admirable (Philippians 4.8).

Nevertheless, the issue was becoming more complex than simple commitment phobia. My girlfriend noticed there were times I sought her permission for things that were obviously not within her authority. For example, when I needed to buy a new watch, I was afraid to do so and needed her approval. Also, there were times when I felt guilty just being with her. Sometimes in the evenings, when I felt accused or blamed for wrongdoing, I would 'shut down' and be unable to function socially. These 'shut down' periods might end in sudden bouts of tears. My girlfriend later described me as one who sounded like a deeply wounded animal.

To make matters worse, the medication was causing me to gain weight, but more importantly, it numbed my feelings. Although the medication helped lower the feelings of anxiety, it also made it difficult for me to process my feelings. It became obvious that both the medication and the spiritual healing sessions had their limitations.

Biblical counselling and therapy

Finally, I sought advice from a more senior pastor who, by God's grace, recommended me to see a Christian counsellor whom he knew to help process my thoughts and emotions and to get to the root of the issue. By this time, I had already been having panic attacks for more than a year. With the counsellor, one of the key issues that we discovered together was the emotional abuse I suffered at the hands of my previous girlfriend.

During my previous two-year relationship, after the first three months of dating 'honeymoon', my then girlfriend subjected me to long bouts of anger. I was held hostage by guilt over my past and considered not good enough to marry her. So whenever she was unhappy, whether it was work, family or relationships, somehow it was linked back to me and my past and I became the main source of responsibility for her dissatisfaction in life. I tried my best to become an ideal boyfriend for her but at times that seemed like an impossible goal. Slowly, she began to cut me off from my friends, saying they would be a bad influence on me. Then negative thoughts about my own family were planted, making her the victim of my family's 'dysfunction'.

> My girlfriend later described me as one who sounded like a deeply wounded animal.

She also used her status as a Christian and her Bible knowledge to claim superiority over me as I wasn't a Christian then. Her final trump card was always to use my past sins as a leverage for her to manipulate me into feelings of guilt, whether true or false. Frivolous mistakes and matters would be magnified into imagined scenarios

of life-and-death proportion. At times, I would be made guilty for causing her to have anger and suicidal thoughts. These tantrums and guilt-trip sessions would last more than a day. Sometimes I was not allowed to even eat my dinner or I was shamed in public, or phone calls were made to my mobile throughout the night. After absorbing all the 'verbal bashing', there came a time when my body actually shook in fear as I had to repress all my fears, mixed with anger at being shouted and screamed at.

Looking back, I had two reasons/motivations to remain in the relationship. Firstly, we did have happy times together, despite the bouts of anger. There was no doubt she cared for me, showed me genuine concern, patiently tried to teach me the Bible and gave me space where I could find out more about Christianity, etc. This gave me hope that perhaps one day I would not cause her to be angry with me and when I became a Christian she would be able to forgive my past. The hope of being able to relive those happy moments kept me from leaving the relationship.

Secondly, because I did not believe in God then, I gave all authority over my life to her, and she became my god. Thus she became the final authority on all matters of my life. So leaving her would be tantamount to betrayal. There was an 'unseen leash' around me. Even when both of us had moved on to new relationships, I would feel guilty starting a new one.

With the Christian counsellor, I managed to process my past relationship. Through role-playing, I was able to express my repressed anger and pain. My body shook with emotions during those sessions, confirming that the emotional abuse was the main cause of my pain and anxiety. Even then, at times I still felt guilty when sharing with the counsellor. I was worried that I had exaggerated the past and painted my previous girlfriend too negatively.

The power of the Word

The counsellor also helpfully pointed out some Bible verses to help me overcome my anxiety attacks: "He is before all things, and in him all things hold together" (Colossians 1.17). Whenever a wave of panic attacks started, I learned to breathe in deeply and recall that in Jesus, all things hold together. Colossians taught that Jesus not only created the entire universe and all life forms; He also held together all things. He is both the Creator and Sustainer of all things. All events are held in His sovereign hands. Even when we are caught in unpleasant situations, we know that God is still in control and will see us through.

I remember at one point in my journey, I experienced a relapse. I really wanted to give up my struggles and not continue in my relationship with my then girlfriend. The feelings of guilt and pain were too strong and the fear of commitment overwhelmed me. I got down on my knees by my bed and told God I couldn't take this struggle anymore. It had been already two years. Just as my knees touched the ground, my mobile phone received a message with the words, "If God brings you to it, he will bring you through it". I later discovered that the message came from France, from an old friend who was living there. She told me later she had randomly sent out this message to ten of her friends as part of a "chain mail" to get "good luck". God showed me that despite the difference in time zone, vast geographical distance and unrelated motivation, the timeliness of the message was a great proof of His complete sovereignty. Since He was in full control, He knew what was happening and He allowed me to go through this for His glory and purpose.

Another verse that greatly helped me was John 3.17, "For God did not send his Son into the world to condemn the world, but to save the world through him". This showed me that God's Son Jesus didn't come to condemn me, but to save me.

After being emotionally abused by someone who shared with me the Bible and its truths, often in condemnation, it was difficult to imagine that God truly loves me. Instead, I often confused God's voice with a tone of perpetual condemnation. When the counsellor showed me John 3.17, I realised that while we stood condemned before God because of our sins, out of His love for us, He came to save us from our sins and not to condemn us.

Knowing that God was on the side of those who believed in Him greatly helped me appreciate His love and separate Him from the voice of the abuser. "If God is for us, who can be against us?" (Romans 8.31) So there is now "no condemnation for those who are in Christ Jesus" (Romans 8.1).

Knowing that God was both on my side and in full control helped me gain courage and faith in Him, and slowly but surely, I was able to stop my medication and started to walk by faith. Knowing I was deeply forgiven by God on the Cross, I found the strength to totally forgive my ex-girlfriend. By setting her free through total forgiveness, I was set free from bondage to both repressed anger and fear of abuse. It also helped me reconcile with my past conflicted feelings of affection for her which were twisted with thorns of pain and fears.

By the end of four years of this journey, with God's strength and love, I managed to move on from my past, overcame my commitment phobia and married the one who stood by me during these years of darkness. She became my loving and supportive wife.

Reflection

After coming out of those years of anxiety attacks, my wife and I always look back and thank God for sustaining the two of us together and for His great healing. Of course, I would not want to go through the pain again, yet those were important years to teach me God's sovereignty, grace, love and faithfulness to sustain me in my faith. Being so helpless in those years with no glimpse of hope at times, the fact that I am still a Christian today is testimony to God's faithfulness.

In addition, I now understand that God made us complex beings, consisting of multiple dimensions in our being — spiritual, physical and emotional. My personal journey showed me that healing requires a holistic approach. Dealing with just one dimension would not have been sufficient. All three came together to help me recover fully as a person. If I had not confessed and repented of my sins and sinful coping mechanisms, I would still be trapped in the vicious cycle of sin and abuse. If I had not taken the medication, I would still be crumbling from the physical effects of the anxiety attacks, and be too weak to have gone for biblical counselling and therapy to address the root issues. But most of all, it is the knowledge that there is a true and living God who walks with me that helps me walk through the valley of the shadow of death (Psalm 23.4).

It has been more than ten years since I first experienced the panic attacks. At times, I still feel weak, especially when interacting with people with uncontrollable anger and who prefer to pin on me the blame for their own failures. Any emotionally healthy person would suffer from such toxic relationships, let alone one who was previously abused. I still go through small periods of minor relapse but God has proven Himself faithful again and again. My weakness continues to keep me humble and helps me appreciate His love and mighty hand in rescuing me, so that I can clearly say, "His grace is sufficient for me" (2 Corinthians 12.9).

> My personal journey showed me that healing requires a holistic approach.

Further Reading

Roy Clements, *Songs of Experience* (Fearn, UK: Christian Focus, 1993).

NHG Psychiatry Workgroup, *A Patient Education Guide to Coping with Anxiety* (Singapore: National Healthcare Group, n.d.).

Addictions

> "'Everything is permissible for me' – but I will not be
> mastered by anything...Do you not know that your body is
> a temple of the Holy Spirit, who is in you, whom you have
> received from God? You are not your own; you were bought
> at a price. Therefore honour God with your body."
> *(1 Corinthians 6.12b, 19–20)*

Addictions: Sin or Sickness?

Some addictions are sinful because the behaviour or mental activity involved are intrinsically sinful. Pornography falls into this category (Matthew 5.27–28; 1 Corinthians 6.18; Ephesians 5.3–5; Colossians 3.5–6). Drug abuse is sinful because of its illegality and the harm it does to one's body which is the temple of the Holy Spirit.

There are other behaviours and mental activities which are alright in moderation but become sinful when they become addictions. These include alcohol, computer games and Facebook(?!). For Christians, the Lordship of Christ means being yielded to His control (Romans

6.11–13), thus to be under the control of any other influence cannot be pleasing to God (1 Corinthians 6.12; Ephesians 5.18). Our bodies and minds do not belong to us to use or abuse as we please. They belong to God (1 Corinthians 6.19–20).

What are some practical implications of this? People caught in the bondage of addiction are sinners as well as victims. There needs to be an acknowledgement of one's addiction as sin before God followed by repentance and confession as part of the rehabilitation process. Indeed, the *Twelve Steps of Alcoholics Anonymous* incorporate this. [23]

The Power of Christ

Since the mid-seventies, I have been associated with different Christian halfway houses in Singapore. I have heard many recovered Christian hardcore addicts testify that without the power of Christ they would not have been able to escape the bondage of drugs. Many had been in and out of detention centres and prisons for ten or more years. They had tried various ways without success. It was only when they gave their lives to Jesus Christ that they were finally able to break free. Even then, many lapsed at least once before becoming finally free. So with addictions, particularly hardcore drugs, Christian spiritual resources, especially the person and power of Christ, can make a vital difference.[24] Support from Christian friends is also important, whether in a halfway house, church cell group or the recovered addict's family members.

Jeff found all this very true in his own life. Having completed his Bible college training, Jeff is now a pastor in a local church where he is overseeing the church's Mercy Ministry. This ministry consists of the Bereavement Ministry, Cancer Support Ministry, Visitation Ministry and the Prison Ministry. Jeff oversees the Bereavement and Prison Ministries. He ministers in Changi

Prison Sunday chapels two Sundays a month as well as in the after-care ministry.

 **Jeff's Testimony**

I started being rebellious at a very young age. I enjoyed the liberty I demanded from my parents. However it had dire consequences on my life. To begin with, I grew to dislike authority: teachers, law-keepers and even my parents. I just wanted to live life my way and not be constrained by any form of structures that may hinder the freedom and hedonistic lifestyle I enjoyed. Consequently, my behaviour deteriorated as did my studies.

At social gatherings, I met and made friends with people older than me. It did not take long for me to be badly influenced by their care-free and care-less attitude. At least we shared something in common which fed my appetite for freedom of expression, so I thought. One thing led to another and I soon found myself indulging in illegal and illicit drugs. After all, it was the hippie era that I grew up in. Like most trends, it was the in-thing to do. Drugs took away the prime of my life.

My first admission to prison for rehabilitation was difficult for several reasons. Firstly, the freedom I enjoyed was taken from me. Subsequently, the luxury of having things as demanded, was curbed to a bare minimum. The last but most important thing to be taken from me was my personhood, my humanity. I became only a digit in the prison system. After experiencing this humbling experience, I vowed to keep my life on the straight and narrow. But it was to no avail. On numerous occasions I was apprehended by the law and sent to prison.

However, something good came out of the last admission. Particularly, I was more than determined to really start life afresh. There were several factors that influenced my wanting to change, but none so important as the liberating truth of the gospel of God. The Good News revealed anew my rebelliousness and the need for forgiveness from God's anger on my wayward ways. And the truth of grace offered me eternal life. It also required that I correctly respond by living for God and not to self. In confession, I asked for God's mercy and grace to be a constant reminder as I re-ordered my God-given life. Hence, I found life to be meaningful and purposeful, even though I still face trials, temptations and disappointments as I embark on this journey of faith. But it was and is to be a meaningful and purposeful journey nonetheless.

Upon release, my continued walk with God found a home in the welcoming and accepting hearts of a cell group and the church where I grew and matured. Being with God's people has played a very big part in my walk with Christ. The preaching and teaching in church helped me grow and apply the knowledge of God in Jesus Christ and I slowly matured to be more like Him.

> The Good News revealed anew my rebelliousness and the need for forgiveness from God's anger on my wayward ways.

Since coming to understand what it means to trust God with my life, I consider it the greatest calling to be able to share my redeemed relationship with a faithful God with those who are still rebelliously ignorant. Now that I am liberated by the gospel, my natural calling is to those in prison. By God's mercy and the power of His Spirit, many will come to the true knowledge of God's salvation in Christ Jesus. Like me, they can live law-abiding lives and be an asset publicly and personally for the furtherance of God's kingdom.

To God be the glory, great things He has done...Amen.

Further Reading

Shawn Wee and Looi Wan Teng, *Yellow Ribbon: True-Life Accounts of Ex-Offenders and Their Second Chance at Life* (Singapore: Marshall Cavendish Editions, 2011).[25]

The annual magazines of Christian halfway houses contain testimonies of lives transformed by Jesus as well as information about their rehabilitation programmes. For details of Christian halfway houses see pages 90 to 92 of this book.

Self-Care

Avoiding Burnout

Symptoms

The signs of burnout tend to be more mental than physical. They can include feelings of:

- Frustration and powerlessness
- Hopelessness
- Being drained of emotional energy
- Detachment, withdrawal, isolation
- Being trapped
- Having failed at what you're doing
- Irritability
- Sadness
- Cynicism (people act out of selfishness and nothing can be done about it).

If you're burning out and the burnout expresses itself as irritability, you might find yourself always snapping at people or making snide remarks about them. If the burnout manifests itself as depression, you might want to sleep all the time or always be 'too tired' to socialise. Your relationships at work and in your personal life may begin to fall apart.

What is the difference between stress and burnout?

Burnout may be the result of unrelenting stress, but it isn't the same as too much stress. Stress, by and large, involves too much: too many pressures that demand too much of you physically and psychologically. Stressed people can still imagine, though, that if they can just get everything under control, they'll feel better. Burnout, on the other hand, is about not enough. Being burned out means feeling empty, devoid of motivation, and beyond caring. People experiencing burnout often don't see any hope of positive change in their situations. If excessive stress is like drowning in responsibilities, burnout is being all dried up.

While you're usually aware of being under a lot of stress, you don't always notice burnout when it happens. The symptoms of burnout — the hopelessness, the cynicism, the detachment from others — can take months to surface. If someone close to you points out changes in your attitude or behaviour that are typical of burnout, listen to that person.

Dr. Archibald Hart, in an article on stress and burnout in the clergy, lists some specific differences between stress and burnout:[26]

Stress	Burnout
Characterised by over-engagement	Characterised by disengagement
Leads to anxiety disorders	Leads to paranoia, detachment, and depression
Emotions are over-reactive	Emotions are blunted
Causes disintegration	Causes demoralisation
Produces urgency and hyperactivity	Produces helplessness and hopelessness
Primary damage is physical	Primary damage is emotional
Exhausts physical energy	Exhausts motivation and drive, ideals and hope
Stress may kill you prematurely, and you won't have enough time to finish what you started.	Burnout may never kill you, but your life may not seem worth living.

Preventing Caregiver Burnout

When it comes to caregiver burnout, the stakes are high, as burned-out caregivers endanger the people they care about. And caregivers are more likely to be truly isolated from others. So the first strategy for preventing burnout as a caregiver is: don't try to do it all alone.

There are services to help caregivers in most communities, and the cost may be based on ability to pay or covered by the care-receiver's insurance. Check to see if these services are available through local agencies:

- Adult day care centres
- Home health aides
- Home-delivered meals
- Respite care
- Transportation services
- Skilled nursing.

The first strategy for preventing burnout as a caregiver is: don't try to do it all alone.

Also, enlist friends and family who live near you to run errands, bring a hot meal, or "baby-sit" the care-receiver so you can have a well-deserved break. Finally, be sure to reward yourself. You deserve it.

Educate yourself

Learn as much about the care-receiver's illness and about how to be a caregiver as you can. The more you know, the more effective you'll be, and the better you'll feel about your efforts.

Join a support group

Find a caregivers' support group. You'll feel better knowing that other people are in the same situation, and their knowledge can be invaluable, especially if they're dealing with the same illness you are.

Know your limits

Be realistic about how much of your time and yourself you can give, set limits, and communicate those limits to doctors, family members and other people involved.

Accept your feelings

You might be angry toward the care-receiver because your care isn't appreciated; because you feel trapped in the position of caregiver; because someone you care about is ill. And then you might feel guilty for being angry. As long as you don't compromise the well-being of the care-receiver, allow yourself to feel what you feel.

Confide in others

Talk to people about what you feel; don't keep your emotions bottled up. This is where the support group comes in, but trusted friends and family members can help too. Best defence against all burnout: Being with other people.

Time to yourself in order to relax is important in reducing stress, but if you are approaching burnout, it's also crucial that you cultivate relationships with other people and spend time socializing with them. Poor relationships and isolation can contribute to burnout, but positive relationships can help prevent or reduce its onset.

Here are some steps you can take to improve your relationships with others:

- Nurture your closest relationships, such as those with your partner, children or friends. These relationships can help restore energy and alleviate some of the psychological effects of burnout, such as feelings of being under-appreciated. Try to put aside what's burning you out and make the time you spend with loved ones positive and enjoyable.

- Develop casual social relationships, on and off site, with people at your workplace. "We do all kinds of things, whether it is getting together to play cards or going out to eat. It gives everyone an opportunity to relax and blow off steam," a teacher wrote to a contributors' site. Just remember to avoid hanging out with negative-minded people who do nothing but complain.

•   Connect with a cause or a community group that is personally meaningful to you. Joining a religious, social, or support group can give you a place to talk to like-minded people about how to deal with daily stress – and to make new friends. If your line of work has a professional association, you can attend meetings and interact with others coping with the same workplace demands.

•   Practice healthy communication. Express your feelings to others who will listen, understand, and not judge. Burnout involves feelings that fester and grow, so be sure to let your emotions out in healthy, productive ways.

In summary, to prevent or recover from burnout, learn to cultivate methods of personal renewal, self-awareness and connection with others, and don't be afraid to acknowledge your own needs and find ways to get your needs met.

How to Survive and End Well[27]

Take care of ourselves so we can more effectively take care of others

When I told the Director of a Nursing Home that Dad, the caregiver, had passed away before Mum, the bedridden care-receiver, she commented, "So often the caregiver goes before the one cared for." As part of flight safety information, cabin crews instruct parents to place oxygen masks on themselves first before attending to their child. This goes against parental instincts. But a parent who has blacked out is of no help to anyone.

In Acts 20.28 the apostle Paul exhorted the Ephesian elders to "Keep watch over yourselves and all the flock of which the Holy Spirit has made you overseers". Paul probably had in mind their life and doctrine (cf 1 Timothy 4.16). However, I believe Paul's exhortation may be extended to cover our overall wellness. If we are unwell, whether physically, emotionally, psychologically, mentally or spiritually, we are less able to help others.

A 'no' is not necessarily a negative

A 'no' to a non-priority facilitates a 'yes' to a priority. Being a Christian (worker) does not oblige us to respond to every call for help or ministry. We may burn out if we do. I remember being asked if I would accept an invitation to speak to a youth group any Saturday in the following year. When I said 'no' the person was naturally surprised and disappointed. Surely I had one Saturday free the following year! I explained I had certain God-given priorities. If I kept saying 'yes' to non-priorities I would not have adequate time for my priorities which, at the time, included writing. Thankfully, he understood and accepted my explanation.

A friend told me of an incident which took place when he was the first full-time General Secretary of a Christian organisation in Singapore. One morning he informed his office manager he would be busy on a very important task and was not to be disturbed. That day happened to be the day for mailing out material to those on the mailing list. Being short-staffed, the office manager was making heavy work of it. Finally he decided to ask the General Secretary to lend a hand despite his previous instruction not to be disturbed. To the office manager's surprise and disappointment, the General Secretary was doing nothing — simply staring into space! Knowing what his office manager would be thinking the General Secretary explained, "My main priority as the first full-time General Secretary is to discern and determine the directions and priorities for our ministry. At this early stage of our ministry it is paramount that I focus on this. No one else is in a position to do this. If I help here and there every time there is a call, I will not be able to give the time and energy that I should to this priority task."

Mark 1.35–39 tells us that after healing and delivering many who had been brought to Him, Jesus retired to a solitary place to pray. The next morning, Peter and the others found Him and told Him everyone was looking for Him, presumably other people who were sick or demon-possessed. There was still much need there but Jesus said, "Let us go to the nearby villages so I can preach there also. That is why I have come." This was Jesus' priority. Certainty of this enabled Him to say no to a non-priority, albeit a very needy non-priority, and yes to His priority. Therefore it is so important to discern our God-given priorities so that we have peace when we say *no* and when we say *yes*.

I am not a saviour, Jesus is! I am but His instrument, His servant

I once was caught up in a deep family conflict between a retired father and his grown-up children. It reached the stage where I felt a successful resolution of the conflict rested solely with me. I spent much time and energy trying to resolve the conflict. Not surprisingly, symptoms of over-stress appeared. I began to reflect on the situation. I wrote down my reflections in a pastoral letter.

> Once again I have been experiencing the familiar symptoms of stress despite having counselled others how to deal with stress! What has brought this about? (Among other things) a saviour-complex where I think a satisfactory solution rests with me. But I am not a saviour, I am only an instrument of God for Him to use as He wills. I must recognise my limitations and the boundaries of my responsibilities. I don't have to take on board unnecessary guilt for not being

able to accomplish something that is not my responsibility or is beyond my ability. My responsibility is to be an instrument, not a Saviour.

The apostle Paul understood this when he wrote, "What, after all, is Apollos? And what is Paul? Only servants, through whom you came to believe – as the Lord has assigned to each his task. I planted the seed, Apollos watered it, but God made it grow" (1 Corinthians 3.5-6).

"I am what I am by the grace of God"

In *Do You Sometimes Feel Like a Nobody* by Tim Stafford,[28] one story that impressed and touched me very much was about the unexpected visitor who turned up at a Christian summer camp for kids. He was an eighteen-year-old cerebral palsy victim who wanted to accompany the six boys he had driven to the camp. When he was born, that part of his brain that controls the small muscles of the body was damaged so he couldn't talk or walk right. He couldn't control or co-ordinate his movements and he wasn't good looking. Halfway through the camp he asked for a chance to say a few words to all the campers. Let me extract, beginning with the camp commandant's response to his request...

> "What are you going to do if I let you talk and you begin to drool and everybody's looking at you and they can hardly understand you? What are you going to do if some good-looking guy all the girls have been hanging around like flies all week stands up and says, 'Man, I don't have to put up with this. I'm getting out of here?' What are you going to do if the guy leaves?" He said, "Bob, that's not my problem. That's his problem." That settled it. "Okay, you can talk to the kids." The next morning he got up in front of the group right after breakfast. He tried to hold his hands still but he was nervous. When he finally got his composure, his first

words were: "I am what I am by the grace of God." Everything suddenly became dead silent. There wasn't a person in the room who wasn't hit by that statement. There he stood with that twisted body saying, "I am what I am by the grace of God." He continued, "You know, God doesn't just love the people who eat right, because I can't. God doesn't just love the people who can walk right, because I can't. God loves me just as much as he loves you, and he made me just as unique as he made you."

This really spoke to me personally because I used to suffer from a deep inferiority complex. If God loves and accepts me as I am (in Christ), who am I to reject myself. Let me share something of how I felt at the time. I was convinced, for example, that I would never have a girlfriend. I reasoned like this: If I were a girl would I want myself for a boyfriend? No way! That was exactly how I felt. I was even afraid to ask my friends at University to join me for lunch. Thus I would often be found eating sandwiches by myself on the front lawn of Sydney University. I dared not ask my friends to join me for I was convinced that no one enjoyed my company. I thought of myself as being imprisoned in an egg shell, unable to break out. The inferiority complex did not go away when I became a Christian. It was still with me when I was leader of the young adult's group.

Because of my inferiority complex and self-consciousness, I would either be more withdrawn and retiring than I should be, or try to show off to gain attention. Either way, I felt like a goof afterwards. My low self-esteem meant I was excessively affected by criticism or praise. I think of those plastic air-filled figures with a weighted bottom. Even a gentle push can cause them to rock back and forth. I was like that. A word of criticism or praise would send me swaying to and fro.

Once, when my daughter Michelle was about five, she asked me if she sang alright. Now and then she would stray from the tune and her older brother and sister would quickly let her know! I told her she sang alright – given that she was trying her best and her singing voice had yet to stabilise. Some time afterwards, she went a bit off key again and drew the usual unhelpful comments from her brother and sister. Her response to their  "God loves me just as much as he loves you, and he made me just as unique as he made you."

heckling was, "Anyway Daddy says I sing alright, so there!" What her father thought of her counted more than what others, including her brother and sister, thought of her. What my heavenly Father thinks of me should matter more to me than what others think. The Lord's healing here has given me great freedom in this area. I am no longer a 'slave' to the opinions and comments of others in terms of what I think I should or should not do and be. What matters most is that I rest secure and find my stability in the Lord's acceptance of me in Christ. This leads me to the fifth point.

Justification by faith through grace

"[For] all have sinned and fall short of the glory of God, and are justified freely by his grace through the redemption that came by Christ Jesus" (Romans 3.23–24). A seminary principal said the main problem with missionaries in an Asian country he visited was they did not understand justification by faith nor the application of justification by faith to their ongoing Christian life and ministry. They failed to appropriate the truth that God accepted them only on the basis of what Christ did on the Cross and never on the basis of what they did or didn't do. As a recent song says, "Nothing that I do can make Him love me more, can make Him love me less". This does not mean God will never be disappointed or displeased with me. But it does mean His love and acceptance of me remains unchanged. Here are four practical implications of this truth.

Firstly, justification by faith through grace applies, not only to the moment of conversion, but also to one's ministry and the whole of one's Christian life! We understand God's initial acceptance of us was wholly through His grace appropriated by faith. But in our Christian life and ministry we think God's continuing acceptance and love now depends on our pleasing Him, on our obedience, on what we do or don't do. We may not even be aware this is what is happening.

I think of the experiences of two of my former students. One was very driven when she did her assignments, always striving to score A's. I learned that her mother had died when she was young. She yearned for her father's love and attention. It seemed her father paid attention to her when she did well in her studies. So her drivenness in her studies was fuelled by her need for recognition and approval. The other, one of three brothers, had a father who only praised his sons if they scored in the top three of their class. Not only did this result in insecurity and drivenness in their studies, it also led to an unhealthy rivalry among the brothers. God is not at all like these two fathers. God's acceptance, approval and love is not contingent on how well we do. We need to understand that God's love for us is grounded in what Jesus did on the Cross and that is something that is unchanging. So His love and acceptance of us is constant and unchanging.

> God's acceptance, approval and love is not contingent on how well we do.

Secondly, justification by faith through grace leaves no room for pride or boasting. It reminds me that my acceptance by God is never on the basis of anything good or even extra-good that I do. This is as true of my ongoing Christian life as it was of my conversion! If I really knew this truth experientially, my life would be characterised by thankfulness, not self-satisfaction nor self-congratulations nor disappointment when praise is not forthcoming from others.

Thirdly, justification by faith through grace should keep me from undue discouragement and depression when I believe I have failed God. This was driven home to me many years back in my contact with recovered Christian drug addicts who had lapsed and gone back to drugs. Their deep sense of shame and failure hindered their coming back for help. They felt their failure and backsliding had disqualified them in the sight of God and forfeited any right to be accepted back by God. This is wrong thinking. God's acceptance of us is never on the basis of our own righteousness which will fail, but on the basis of Christ's righteousness which never fails! When we sin and fail we may break our fellowship with God and lose our peace but we do not lose our justification or cease to be sons and daughters of God.

I sometimes illustrate this through a double-handed grip where I grip a person's arm and he simultaneously grips mine. Suppose he releases his grip and lets go. Will I, representing God, let go? Not at all. God holds on to us on the basis of Christ's unfailing righteousness which has been credited to us. What a gloriously comforting assurance it is to know that God's acceptance of me does not depend upon my frail, imperfect righteousness but on Christ's perfect righteousness.

Someone once told me of an Anglican minister who would don his surplice (a white full-length gown/robe) to perform his ministerial duties. Apparently under the pristine, white surplice he might sometimes be wearing shorts and slippers! But the congregation would only see the surplice. Analogously, when God looks at us, He sees us clothed in the righteousness of the Lord Jesus Christ which covers the dirt and stain of our sin.

Finally, a proper understanding of justification by faith through grace should banish apathy and nominalism. One of the charges levelled against Paul and later against Martin Luther was that this teaching would lead to nominalism and would open the way for licentious behaviour. When people are told they are justified by faith and not by works they may not be motivated to do good works. They may even exploit God's grace. However, the opposite was true in Martin Luther's day. Justification by faith through grace was liberating and energising. It freed men and women from their sense of guilt, pessimism and resignation with regard to living a God-pleasing life. It freed and motivated them to do an abundance of good works, in loving, grateful response to God's wonderful grace!

My early years at university were marked by failure. The Lord drew me to Himself in that period. Finding new purpose in life, I applied myself to my studies. However, I feared I was heading for a second failure in Chinese. I told my mother about this. I felt I owed her this as she and my father had sacrificed much to pay for my University studies. I wanted her to scold me but she didn't. She just said quietly, "That's okay, John. Just try your best and if you do fail we will pay for you to try again next year."

What was my response? I could have rejoiced (not outwardly of course) and, with relief, cease studying Chinese since I was going to fail anyway. That was not how I responded. I was so overwhelmed by my mother's love and acceptance of me and my failures that I found myself liberated and energised to apply myself to my Chinese. Against the odds, I passed! That incident gave me some insight into what ought to happen when we truly grasp what justification by grace through faith really is.

A proper understanding and grasp of justification by faith through grace ought to have a tremendously liberating effect on us. It ought to motivate us to desire growth in righteousness as our grateful, love-response to the Lord for His wonderful unconditional grace to us. It ought to lift from us that unhealthy sense of duty that can weigh so heavily upon us and replace it with joyful gratitude in our care of others.

Reflections on being diagnosed with a serious, potentially terminal illness

In March 2006 I was diagnosed with Motor Neurone Disease. I became very reflective and sober when I read some of the literature my daughter sent me. Fifty percent of those with MND die within fourteen months of diagnosis! Those with the most common form, ALS (Lou Gehrig's disease), normally die within two to five years. [29]

I am very thankful to the Lord that the diagnosis of MND did not shake my confidence that God is sovereign, that He is in control and that these developments are in His hands. I am very thankful for the peace and calm I enjoyed. I wasn't trying to be heroic or stoic. Peace and calm were just there. It helped me to understand others who, for example, could meet news of terminal cancer with peace and calm.

Various passages of Scripture became very meaningful during this period. Not surprisingly the first passage that I meditated on was Romans 8.28. God is working for my good in all things! A related passage is Psalm 31.14-15, "But I trust in you, O LORD; I say, 'You are my God.' My times are in your hands". My times are indeed in God's hands. My lot, my circumstances are in His hands.

As people came to know about my condition I began to receive various emails. One that really struck a chord in me came from my wife Frances' close friend in Hong Kong: "I suppose at this stage you just have to wait it out to see what the second opinion in Sydney says. Aren't we glad our Lord knows what He is doing. We are here only to carry out His plans and purposes. With Him we can face any 'tomorrows', come what may."

Why was this on just the right wavelength for me? "We are here only to carry out His plans and purposes." How true. This is precisely it. When I understand this, I am much more able to acknowledge God's sovereignty even in difficult and painful situations. It is not that my life belongs to me and it is my prerogative to choose how I shall live my life, for example, to decide how much of my life I want to give to serving God. No! All my life belongs to God. I am here simply for the Lord to fulfil His purposes in and through me. Awareness of this has brought great freedom and 'relaxation' in my ministry. I just rest and yield myself to the Lord to fulfil His purposes in and through me.

Further Reading

Institute of Mental Health, *Caregivers' Guide*, 3rd ed. (Singapore: Institute of Mental Health, September 2008).

A Special Note on
Mental Illness and
Bible Study[30]

Mental illness affects the way a person may interpret and apply Bible passages. Depending on the type and severity of the mental illness, the interpretation and application will vary.

For example, Galatians 5.22–23 lists the fruit of the Spirit. A person with severe depression may interpret the lack of feeling these qualities as evidence of not having the Spirit and therefore of being of the flesh. But it may be that it is the depressed mood which colours their thinking and feelings negatively which then leads to self-condemnation despite encouragement from others. Similarly, someone with a generalised anxiety disorder and panic attacks may believe they lack faith because they feel mainly anxious about most things in their lives.

Those with psychosis may take the exchange between Jesus and the rich young man in Matthew 19.16–30 as wholly applied to them and literally sell all they own and leave their families.

Therefore it is helpful if Bible study leaders are aware that those who are suffering from a mental illness may interpret and apply the Bible inappropriately. There have been times when sufferers have preferred a one-on-one Bible study which allows them to clarify and work through the Bible in a way uniquely suited to their condition.

Christian Resources

At times life can be a real roller-coaster,
but "God is our refuge and strength, an ever-present
help in trouble. Therefore we will not fear, though
the earth give way and the mountains fall into
the heart of the sea, though its waters roar and foam
and the mountains quake with their surging."
(Psalm 46.1–3)

Select Annotated Bibliography

General
Gordon Fee, *The Disease of the Health and Wealth Gospels* (Vancouver, Canada: Regent College Publishing, 1985).

The author, an ordained pastor of the Assemblies of God and a New Testament scholar and teacher, presents an evangelical position on this issue.

Patricia Yap, Daryl Chow, Sharon Lu, Brenda Lee (eds.), *Mind this Voice: The Write to Recovery* (Singapore: Institute of Mental Health, 2011).

Personal stories and lessons about recovery from mental health concerns. Written by sufferers with accompanying inputs by their therapists.

Psychosis

Harris Ng, *Recovered Grace: Schizophrenia* (Singapore: Harris Ng, 2005).

This is an inspiring and informative book. Harris, a believer, shares with us his sixteen-year struggle with paranoid schizophrenia which included four relapses and the painful process of recovery each time. We gain valuable insights as Harris shares about the lessons he learned from his relapses.

NHG Psychiatry Workgroup, *A Patient Education Guide to Living with Psychosis* (Singapore: National Healthcare Group, n.d.).

This series of eight-page booklets by the NHG Psychiatry Workgroup gives helpful summarised information of mental illnesses and their treatment.

NHG Psychiatry Workgroup, *A Patient Education Guide to Living with Schizophrenia* (Singapore: National Healthcare Group, n.d.).

Rita Goh, *Back from the Brink of Insanity* (Singapore: Rita Goh, 2005).

Rita provides a very transparent account of the confusion, disabilities, bizarre behaviour and thinking that her paranoid schizophrenia caused her, as well as the toll this took on her loved ones. She also chronicles her gradual, full recovery. In the preface she acknowledges the prayers and support of her church members.

Robert Solomon, *Living in Two Worlds: Pastoral Responses to Possession in Singapore* (Frankfurt, Germany: Peter Lang International Academic Publishers, 1994).

Robert Solomon, a former Bishop of the Methodist Church in

Singapore, is a doctor, pastor and theological teacher. This book is based on his doctoral thesis for Edinburgh University.

Mood Disorders

Kay Redfield Jamison, *An Unquiet Mind: A Memoir of Moods and Madness* (London, UK: Picador, 1997).

Dr Jamison, Professor of Psychiatry at the John Hopkins Medical School, has written an amazing book detailing her journey with a severe bipolar disorder that took her through episodes of severe mania (to the point of insanity) and depression. I not only learned much about bipolar disorder and its treatment; I was also able to 'feel' much. Her writing style makes for an engaging read.

Roy Clements, *Songs of Experience* (Fearn, UK: Christian Focus, 1993).

Chapter 1 is a very insightful, helpful discussion of depression based on Psalms 42–43. Very encouraging and reassuring for Christians who suffer from depression and feel the stigmatised.

Anxiety Disorders

NHG Psychiatry Workgroup, *A Patient Education Guide to Coping with Anxiety* (Singapore: National Healthcare Group, n.d.).

Addictions

Shawn Wee and Looi Wan Teng, *Yellow Ribbon: True-Life Accounts of Ex-Offenders and Their Second Chance at Life* (Singapore: Marshall Cavendish Editions, 2011).

As I read the accounts in this book, I noticed that a significant factor in a number of the people overcoming and breaking free from their past was the part played in their lives by the Lord Jesus and by Christians. I refer you to the following (the page numbers in brackets indicate where they write about their Christian experience): Hanniel (42–43); William (52–53); Tony (68–70); Michael (87–91); Samueal

Kumar (97–98); Jimmy (115).

The annual magazines of Christian halfway houses contain testimonies of lives transformed by Jesus as well as information about their rehabilitation programmes. For details of Christian halfway houses see pages 90 to 92 of this book.

Self-Care
Institute of Mental Health, *Caregivers' Guide*, 3rd ed. (Singapore: Institute of Mental Health, September 2008).

Endnotes

1   Martyn Lloyd-Jones, *Preaching and Preachers* (London, UK: Hodder and Stoughton, 1971).

2   Ibid., 37. Here are extracts from three communications I received following, respectively, a class I taught and two sermons I preached:
    "Thank you for your teaching tonight. I've been battling bouts of panic and near depression because I was overly focussed on work and your sharing about excellence and pleasing God was a much needed timely reminder for me. I left your class with a burden lifted and a clear mind....Your one lesson has really altered my perspective on work and I have spent time with the Lord on this."
                                                                    ~A sister from Singapore

    "I thought I'll drop you a note to thank you for the worship service today as I found the whole service including your sermon so relevant and encouraging to me and I wanted to share with you how God looks after me. I know I should not be surprised but it never ceases to amaze me how God does this. After a particularly traumatic event in your life and within a 24-hour turn around time God explains why. Truly amazing!"

~*A brother from Sydney*

"Thank you for the sermon today. It struck me very deeply, in particular the parts about God stretching us and about inferiority. I believe God speaks to us in the times we need to hear it.

I have been quite down for a while, and I'm still not sure why. It got to the point I thought of giving up my counselling course because the self-reflection gets so painful, and I started doubting my motivation and purpose in taking this course. How can I hope to help others when I sometimes can't accept myself? And especially when I have not resolved my past and present issues. What makes it feel worse is the realization that my low self esteem is tied inextricably with pride and self centredness. Last night I broke down and told my husband that the course is a big mistake. Today when you shared about your son's swimming lessons, and your experience with feelings of inferiority, it felt like a reminder to persevere. Thank you for sharing with such honesty. It was very encouraging."

~*A sister from Singapore*

Other pastors would have received similar letters.

3   Larry Crabb, *Effective Biblical Counselling* (Grand Rapids, USA: Zondervan, 1977), 163–191.

4   John Ting, *Living Biblically in Marriage and at Home* (Singapore: Landmark Books, 2009).

5   Ibid., 148.

6 The following is extracted from Harris Ng, *Recovered Grace: Schizophrenia* (Singapore: Harris Ng, 2005), 46–50.

7 This section on demonism vs psychosis is a slightly revised version of my article, "Satan: The Roaring Lion and the Angel of Light," *Asian Challenge* 18 (1988).

8 Psychology was one of my majors at university. This, plus my more rational Christian background, meant that for quite a while, at the practical level, I did not include the possibility of a demonic cause when I was counselling people. Theologically, I believed in the demonic, of course, but when it came to actual practice it was mostly excluded from my thinking and evaluation when counselling. As a consequence of some personal involvement in exorcism, I now take into practical account the possibility of a demonic cause in relevant situations.

9 Melody has suffered from bipolar illness for over fifteen years so her story should, more correctly, come under Mood Disorders. I included it here because how she begins her story flows naturally on from, and well illustrates, what I wrote on demonism and reaching a right diagnosis. Furthermore, some behaviour and thinking during the manic phase may verge on psychosis.

10 See discussion on pages 5–6, "Healing in the atonement?".

11 Research in the Netherlands has looked at the amount of disability caused by a large number of both physical and mental health problems. 'Disability' refers to the amount of disruption that a health problem causes to a person's ability to work, look after himself and carry on relationships with family and friends. The disability caused by moderate depression is similar to the

disability from relapsing multiple sclerosis, severe asthma, chronic hepatitis B or deafness. See Marlies Stouthard, Marie-Louise Essink-Bot, Gouke Bonsel, et al, "Disability Weights for Diseases: A Modified Protocol and Results for a Western European Region," *European Journal of Public Health* 10 no. 1 (2000): 24–30.

The diagram is taken from Ellen Haller, Jessica Doigny, Carole Farley-Toombs, et al, *Depression: A Common and Treatable Problem* (San Bruno, CA: Krames Communications, 1994), 5.

12 Ronald S. Wallace, *A Study Guide to Elijah and Elisha* (Achimota, Ghana: Africa Christian Press, 1957), 58.

13 Mistakes and poor judgment on my part exacerbated the criticism and misunderstanding.

14 After I taught about depression to a group of Mongolian Christians, they expressed their thanks and relief. Relief that when they now encounter people with depression, they no longer need to 'fight' and battle demonism, which they previously thought was the cause of all depression! This is not to deny that demonism may be a factor in some depression cases. On another occasion I informed a senior Christian lawyer here in Singapore that I suffered from depression. His immediate response was, "Satan?" When I replied that Satan was a possible factor in my depression but I didn't think so, he was quick to retract.

15 Roy Clements, *Songs of Experience* (Fearn, UK: Christian Focus, 1993), 15.

16 A sermon of mine on Christians and depression was edited and rearranged by Mary Yeo-Carpenter to form two articles in *Impact*

August-September 2003, namely "Christians and Depression" and "Downcast Soul".

See also Charles H. Spurgeon, "The Treasury of David," *The Spurgeon Archive*, last modified 2001, http://spurgeon.org/ treasury//ps042.htm.

17 Clements, *Songs of Experience*.

18 In the latter half of 2001 I was put back on an antidepressant and have been on it continuously since.

19 Charles Swindoll notes, "But let's understand that God does not dispense strength and encouragement like a pharmacist fills your prescription. The Lord doesn't promise to give us something to *take* so we can handle our weary moments, He promises us *Himself*. That is all. And that is enough."

"The Savior says: 'Come to me, all who are weary and burdened, and I will give you rest. Take my yoke upon you and learn from me, for I am gentle and humble in heart, and you will find rest for your souls. For my yoke is easy and my burden is light' (Matthew 11.28–30, NIV)...

"In place of our exhaustion and spiritual fatigue, He will give us rest. All He asks is that we come to Him...that we spend a while thinking about Him, meditating on Him, talking to Him, listening in silence, occupying ourselves with Him — totally and thoroughly lost in the hiding place of His presence... When was the last time you came to the Lord, all alone, and gave Him your load of care?

"No wonder you are weary!"

See Charles Swindoll, *Growing Strong in the Seasons of Life* (Portland, USA: Multnomah Press, 1983), 135–137.

20 D.A. Carson, *How Long, O Lord?: Reflections on Suffering and Evil,*
2nd ed. (Nottingham, UK: Inter-Varsity Press, 2006), implies this,
for example:

"Quite frankly, this little book, as I have already hinted, may
not be of assistance to those whose despair is so bleak that they
cannot bring themselves to read, think, and pray. But I shall be
satisfied if it helps some Christians establish patterns and habits
of thought that are so strong that when the hardest questions
batter the soul there is less wavering and more faith, joy, and hope."
(12)

"In the preface I warned you that this is not necessarily a
book that should be read by someone who is going through deep
suffering. It might help some people; most certainly it would not
help others. It is more in the way of preventative medicine: that
is, I have tried to establish some firm structures to help Christians
think about evil and suffering in biblical ways *before* hard days
descend on them." (221)

21 I am less familiar with anxiety disorders. I am grateful for
feedback and comments from Jeannie Koh (former manager and
senior counsellor, NUS Counselling Services. Advisor, MHFA [S]
Executive Committee) and Dr Angelina Chan (Senior Consultant
Psychiatrist, Trauma Recovery and Corporate Solutions [TRaCS],
Changi General Hospital; Chair, MHFA [S] Executive Committee).
Some of the content in this section is derived from them.

22 This is not his real name.

23 I. We admitted we were powerless over alcohol—that our lives had
become unmanageable.
II. Came to believe that a Power greater than ourselves could
restore us to sanity.

III. Made a decision to turn our will and our lives over to the care of God as *we understood Him.*

IV. Made a searching and fearless moral inventory of ourselves.

V. Admitted to God, to ourselves, and to another human being the exact nature of our wrongs.

VI. Were entirely ready to have God remove all these defects of character.

VII. Humbly asked Him to remove our shortcomings.

VIII. Made a list of all persons we had harmed, and became willing to make amends to them all.

X. Made direct amends to such people wherever possible, except when to do so would injure them or others.

XI. Continued to take personal inventory and when we were wrong promptly admitted it.

XII. Sought through prayer and meditation to improve our conscious contact with God, as we understood Him, praying only for knowledge of His will for us and the power to carry that out.

XIII. Having had a spiritual awakening as the result of these Steps, we tried to carry this message to alcoholics, and to practice these principles in all our affairs.

See "The Twelve Steps of Alcoholics Anonymous," *Alcoholics Anonymous World Services,* Inc., 2013, http://www.aa.org/en_pdfs/smf-121_en.pdf.

24 I acknowledge there are former hardcore addicts who have broken free from drugs without the help and power of Jesus.

25 As I read the stories in this book, I noticed that a significant factor in a number of the people overcoming and breaking free from their past was the part played by Jesus and Christians in their lives. I refer you to the following (the page numbers in brackets indicate

where they write about their Christian experience): Hanniel
(42–43); William (52–53); Tony (68-70); Michael (87–91); Samueal
Kumar (97–98); Jimmy (115).

26 Melinda Smith, M.A., Jeanne Segal, Ph.D., and Robert Segal, M.A.,
"Burnout Prevention and Treatment," *Helpguide.org*, last modified
April 2019, https://www.helpguide.org/articles/stress/burnout-
prevention-and-recovery.htm.

27 This is a slightly revised version of a talk I gave to a group of 'tent-
makers' in an Asian country. They had invited me to speak on
"How to survive in the field". After prayer and reflection I decided
to share some of the principles which have helped me survive and
continue in ministry.

28 Tim Stafford, *Do You Sometimes Feel Like a Nobody* (Wheaton, USA:
Campus Life Books, 1986).

29 Thankfully, my MND has turned out to be a more benign, less
disabling form, which may be God's gracious healing in response
to the prayers of many.

30 I have included this special note because Bible study, whether
individual or group, is such an important part of a Christian's life.
The content is taken verbatim from an email sent to me by
Dr Angelina Chan (Senior Consultant Psychiatrist, Trauma
Recovery and Corporate Solutions [TRaCS], Changi General
Hospital. Chair MHFA [S] Executive Committee).

GRACEWORKS

Graceworks is a publishing and training consultancy based in Singapore, dedicated to promoting spiritual friendship in church and society, and seeing lives transformed through books that present truth for life.

Our desire is for our publications to help people apply biblical truths to the challenges of daily living, thus enabling them to live as genuine disciples of Christ in this complex and challenging world. We also have a particular passion to nurture and publish local Singaporean and South-east Asian authors.

Graceworks also runs talks, seminars and workshops both independently and in partnership with churches and organizations that share our vision — to help enable participants to grow in their capacity to live out relationally healthy lives in the church and in the world.

We deeply value and believe in the power of relationships, so we also spend time "on the ground", training mentors and running mentoring groups to help followers of Jesus grow in Christlikeness.

We pray that God will be able to use our ministry to bless you and we invite you to partner with us.

Our publications can be found on our online store www.graceworks.com.sg, Book Depository, Amazon, Kindle, iBooks and Kobo.